THOUGHTS ON
THE CONSTITUTION

L. S. AMERY

With a new Introduction by
GEOFFREY MARSHALL

LONDON
OXFORD UNIVERSITY PRESS
NEW YORK   TORONTO
1964

Oxford University Press, Amen House, London E.C.4

GLASGOW   NEW YORK   TORONTO   MELBOURNE   WELLINGTON
BOMBAY   CALCUTTA   MADRAS   KARACHI   LAHORE   DACCA
CAPE TOWN   SALISBURY   NAIROBI   IBADAN   ACCRA
KUALA LUMPUR   HONG KONG

First published in 1947
Second edition in 1953
and reprinted in 1956
First issued in OXFORD PAPERBACKS 1964

PRINTED IN GREAT BRITAIN

THOUGHTS ON
THE CONSTITUTION

CONTENTS

INTRODUCTION

L. S. AMERY was born in 1873 and died in 1955. After Harrow and Balliol he became exposed at an early stage in his career to the influences, academic and otherwise, of All Souls. The Warden, when Amery was elected a prize fellow in 1897, was Sir William Anson, then putting his *Law and Custom of the Constitution* into its third edition. Professor A. V. Dicey, another of Amery's colleagues, was also in the midst of his labours—'spluttering knowledge and wisdom through an untidy white beard'.[1] Subsequently Amery served as a member of Parliament for more than thirty years, and was, at various times, a member of *The Times* editorial staff, Assistant Secretary to the War Cabinet, Colonial Secretary, Secretary of State for Dominion Affairs, First Lord of the Admiralty and Secretary of State for India and for Burma.

The literature of twentieth-century constitutional practice has not, it must be admitted, been greatly augmented by the writings of practising politicians. Most of them have had neither the time nor inclination to contribute to political science more than their memoirs, in which attention tends to be focused less upon institutions than upon the singular force of the author's personality. Asquith and Churchill perhaps provide exceptions and Lords Attlee and Morrison have more recently supplied considered accounts of the political events of the post-war period. Amery's Chichele lectures may also be added to the canon. They were delivered in 1946 and composed at a period when both

[1] Amery, *My Political Life*, Vol. I, p. 64.

Commonwealth and domestic affairs had reached a critical point of development. In 1953 he was able to take note of events during the Attlee and Churchill administrations. A decade later, in an election year when the working of a number of traditional institutions is under review, many of Amery's questions about the machinery of central government remain pertinent. In a brief introduction attention can most usefully be drawn to those issues which remain open and to those where developments in law or practice since 1953 have modified the force of Amery's arguments.

In the opening lecture, 'The Essential Nature of the Constitution', some emphasis is laid upon the view that the personal power of the monarchy has never been abrogated or its precise limits defined. Perhaps this is putting matters a shade too high. A good deal depends upon what is understood by 'personal'. But it is true that the role of the Crown in the choice of a Prime Minister and in the consideration of a dissolution of Parliament may still from time to time be counted something more than a matter of form and ceremony. Amery does not of course deny that the use of the prerogative is, whatever the theory, substantially based upon the advice of those politicians whom the Crown chooses to consult and who take care to make their views known. Indeed Amery believed that an intervention of his own had a good deal to do with Mr. Baldwin's finding himself Prime Minister in 1923. In his autobiography he relates that after Salisbury had advised Lord Stamfordham that Curzon should be sent for, he (Amery) remonstrated with him and was told that if he felt strongly that the decision would be unpopular with the party as a whole he had better go

and talk to Stamfordham himself. Amery and Bridgeman thereupon set off and seeing at a distance the
King's Private Secretary emerging from his door in
St. James's Palace 'we ran and caught him up and
walked with him into St. James's Park. There we held
him for a quarter of an hour or more, putting our point
of view before him. This was quite new to him.'[1] It
would be pleasant to believe that Lord Curzon's call to
office was so dramatically averted but the more detailed
account which is given in Mr. Robert Blake's biography
of Bonar Law[2] puts a more complex air upon the
transaction.

Whatever the causal efficacy of the various performers
and their advice on this occasion, we may agree with
Amery's view that the episodes of 1923 did not in themselves disqualify members of the upper house for Prime
Ministerial office. Since the power to disclaim a peerage
has been introduced, however, the question whether any
such convention about the office of Prime Minister
existed between the incumbency of Lord Salisbury and
that of Lord Home (as he then was) seems likely to
remain an academic one.

The part played by Queen Elizabeth II in 1957 and
1963 in selecting a Prime Minister from the available
members of the Conservative Party illustrates both that
the Crown is in some sense bound to act upon principle,
precedent and advice and that some freedom exists as to

[1] *My Political Life*, Vol. 2, p. 260. For this somewhat athletic intervention Amery's Balliol training had prepared him well. After bump
suppers 'my forte . . . was hopping on one leg, at which I could beat all
comers down a hundred yards or more of the garden path'. (Ibid., Vol. 1,
p. 44.)

[2] *The Unknown Prime Minister: The Life and Times of Andrew Bonar Law
1858–1923*, pp. 516–27.

the exact quarter in which advice is sought. That freedom would be less with a Labour administration in office, since a retiring Prime Minister's successor would be elected by the Parliamentary Party. The discretion which the Crown is still capable of exercising may also be illustrated by the events of 1950–51. George VI was carefully advised as to his constitutional right to refuse a further dissolution of Parliament immediately after the election of 1950. Amery argues that the right of a Prime Minister to demand a dissolution is not established by the fact that no dissolution has been refused for over a century. He adds that in 1926, he had, as Secretary of State, declined to advise or instruct the Governor of New South Wales in regard to the exercise by him of the royal prerogative. It may be recalled also, by way of illustration of the diverse uses to which the prerogative of the Crown may be put that in 1954 the Governor-General of Pakistan was able with its aid to dissolve the Pakistan constituent assembly and resolve a political and legal crisis.

In his discussion of the House of Commons and of the machinery of cabinet government, Amery's survey covers a number of issues which remain intractable in the 1960s, though perhaps one or two of the forebodings reasonably felt in the 1940s now seem misplaced. The case, for example, which Amery makes for some form of functional representation in the House of Commons is not today a popular one and the expressed need may have been met, at least in part, by the central role played in post-war politics by organized interest groups. Again, the fear of an ever-mounting flood of delegated legislation has receded since 1950. Whilst the total of all forms of statutory instruments has remained fairly steady over the past decade there has been a noticeable decline in the annual total of instruments of general application and the work of the scrutiny committees of both Houses is generally accounted effective. In a number of ways what Lord Hewart saw as the 'New Despotism' of departments has been moderated by statute and administrative practice. The serious constitutional anomaly resulting from the subject's inability to sue the Crown in tort as of right was in the main eliminated by the Crown Proceedings Act of 1947. The untidy procedures of administrative tribunals and ministerial inquiries were investigated by the Franks Committee and have been shaped into a greater uniformity by the Tribunals and Inquiries Act of 1958 and the regulations made under it. A Council on Tribunals set up by the same legislation has the duty of keeping the machinery of administrative adjudication under review and in procedural matters is developing a useful complaints jurisdiction which may yet be extended. Another thoroughly respectable and somewhat delayed reform which is advocated in *Thoughts on the Constitution* reached the statute book with the Life Peerages Act of 1958, whilst the decline of the Lords as a serious political institution has been advanced still further by the provision for renunciation made in 1963 and the concerted (though variously motivated) exertions of Mr. Wedgewood-Benn, Mr. Quintin Hogg and Sir Alexander Douglas-Home.

With a Cabinet of twenty-three members in 1963 the theme of Amery's chapter on cabinet organization continues to hold the attention of both politicians and academic critics. Neither category has favoured Amery's proposal of a small non-departmental cabinet of policy

makers. The arguments for and against it may be
compared by setting alongside each other Amery's third
chapter with the discussion of Cabinet structure in
Professor Harold Laski's *Reflections on the Constitution*
published in 1951. There Laski maintained the view
expressed in his earlier writings that a Cabinet of this
type was 'built upon a theory of the possibility of
separating policy from administration which is un-
workable except under the pressure of such an urgency
as war'.[1] On the other hand it is plain that no immutable maxim of political wisdom dictates that the
natural unit of central policy making is an assembly of
twenty or more. Churchill experimented in 1951 with
supervisory ministers whose administrative as distinct
from parliamentary success remains insufficiently
documented. All post-war Prime Ministers, moreover,
have found it necessary to make extensive use of Cabinet
committees and in varying degrees have felt the need
for a body of confidants or advisers more intimate or
congenial than the whole Cabinet. An informal inner
Cabinet is an established unofficial convenience, and
informal conveniences with us have a habit of turning
into formal institutions. The members of such a group,
however, are less likely to be 'a general staff freed from
administration' than the heads of the most important
existing departments or ministers in direct administrative control of any new conglomerations of departments
that time, chance or deliberation may bring about.

In his final chapter in 1946 Amery turned to the
nature and evolution of the Commonwealth. With
reason he was able to speak of the British or Britannic
Commonwealth and to say of it that the Crown was its

[1] Laski, *Parliamentary Government in England*, 1938, p. 248.

'symbol of partnership and focus of common loyalty'. The common Crown gave 'to the whole commonwealth a constitutionally indissoluble unity which is as essential a 'part of its constitution as the absolute independence and equality of its several partners'. By 1953 the keystone of the Commonwealth constitutional arch was no longer in place. Burma had chosen independence outside the Commonwealth and India, whilst remaining a member, had ceased to acknowledge allegiance to the Crown. Elizabeth II had acquired a new title and capacity as 'Head of the Commonwealth' set out in the Royal Titles Act, 1953. Amery's post-script written in that year speaks of the 'somewhat metaphysical controversy as to the divisibility of the Crown' and contends that despite post-war developments there remained a 'single indivisible historic crown following a single principle of succession and playing a more or less identical part in each constitution'. Perhaps it may be said that such formal truth as there may be in this proposition is fighting a losing battle against political reality.

In the decade since 1953 independence legislation has increased and is increasing the membership of the Commonwealth association, along with the possible permutations of status now available to territories formerly dependent upon the British Crown. It is possible now to have sovereign independence with or without Commonwealth membership and with or without republican status. It was possible for the Malayan Federation to choose membership plus allegiance to a monarch who is not the British monarch. It would presumably be possible (with the co-operation of the Westminster Parliament) to remain one of the Queen's realms after retiring from or being deprived of Commonwealth member status—a fact which has engaged the attention of Commonwealth citizens in Southern Rhodesia. Expulsion from the Commonwealth by a majority vote of the members, if it were to occur, would not in itself have any effect in removing Commonwealth citizenship as defined in the British Nationality Act of 1948. As the withdrawal of South Africa indicated, the rules which regulate admission to and continued membership of the Commonwealth association are coming in practice to rest upon a requirement of majority approval and therefore to divorce the question of member status from that of constitutional autonomy *vis-à-vis* the United Kingdom.

In 1953 Amery saw the Commonwealth as an interlocking entity which despite its altered juristic character might still sensibly be regarded as a unit for economic and defence purposes. Between what remains of that possibility and the forces urging the United Kingdom into co-operation or formal association with its European neighbours the 1960s and 1970s must still decide.

November 1963   GEOFFREY MARSHALL

FOREWORD TO SECOND EDITION

WHEN the four Chichele lectures which made up the original edition of the present work were composed in 1946, our constitutional system had for many years been relatively stable, both in its domestic and in its Commonwealth aspects. At home there had been no direct constitutional controversy since the relations of the two Houses of Parliament were fixed by the 1911 Parliament Act. The ever increasing burden of work upon both Cabinet and the House of Commons was creating problems urgently calling for a remedy, but without, so far, directing public attention to any definite solution. In the Commonwealth the principles embodied in the Constitutional Report of the 1926 Imperial Conference and in the Statute of Westminster had stood the test both of the abdication crisis of 1936 and of the Second World War, and only seemed to need further development in the direction of practical co-operation to meet the economic problems of the post-war situation.

The six years that have passed since then have witnessed changes more significant than any which had taken place in the preceding generation. In the United Kingdom the still important power of delay left to the House of Lords by the 1911 Act has been, to all practical intents and purposes, eliminated. The nationalization of a whole series of major industries has added yet further to the overwork of the House of Commons, while creating new problems of ministerial and parliamentary responsibility to which no clear answer has yet been given. In the Commonwealth the hypothetical question of the right of secession has been, not only accepted as a constitutional principle, but positively carried into effect by Eire and Burma. Even more significant in its possibilities, the Commonwealth has been extended to cover an independent Republic which excludes from its constitution the Crown and the status of British subject derived from it, while acknowledging the Queen as the symbolic Head of the Commonwealth. In consonance with this change what was once a common citizenship based on a common allegiance has been replaced by a series of national citizenships, together with a measure of interchangeable citizen privileges varying in each Realm of the Commonwealth—to use the new constitutional designation.

These developments have been much too important and far-reaching to allow of their character and extent being dealt with by the mere addition of footnotes to the original text. On the other hand it is obvious that we are still far from having achieved finality. The nationalization of our industries has, at this moment, been partially reversed. But it is by no means certain where the eventual equilibrium between State and private industry will be established. The long delayed reform of the House of Lords, now seriously envisaged, may open up the wider question of dealing with the increasingly urgent need of relieving the congestion of parliamentary work. Behind the problem of reconciling Asia to the Commonwealth, there looms, on the one hand, the even more difficult problem of Africa, and, on the other, that of the relation of the Commonwealth, as a whole, or in respect of its several parts, to Europe and to the United States. In these conditions any attempt to embody the changes of the last few years in the main text of the original work could not have been satisfactory, and might soon have been out of date. I have, therefore, adopted the simpler solution of merely adding a chapter of postscript, bringing the situation up to date. How long it will serve that purpose remains to be seen.

April 1953   L. S. AMERY

I

THE ESSENTIAL NATURE OF THE CONSTITUTION

THE British Constitution has never been set out in a written document reflecting the political theories of a particular group of men or the prepossessions of a particular age. It includes some memorable declaratory and statutory milestones of its historic evolution, from Magna Carta to the Statute of Westminster. But some of its most important features are no part of its formal and legal structure and have little other sanction beyond use and precedent. It is only in quite recent years that our legislative vocabulary has even acknowledged the existence of such vital and long-established elements as the Cabinet and the Prime Minister.[1] The whole, like the law of the land of which it is a part, is a blend of formal law, precedent, and tradition. It is a living structure, shaped by the interaction of individual purposes and collective instincts with changing external circumstances. It has followed the laws of its own growth, and not a preconceived intellectual plan designed to control and confine that growth.[2] There has

[1] The existence of a Prime Minister was for the first time officially recognized in a public document in 1878 in the text of the Treaty of Berlin and by the Court Circular of November 1900. It was mentioned for the first time in a statute when the Chequers Trust was constituted in 1917. The word 'Cabinet' appeared for the first time on the notice paper of the House of Commons in 1900. The Cabinet as such has no statutory existence, though an oblique reference to it appears in the Ministers of the Crown Act of 1937.

[2] 'While the mechanical contrivances of political inventors have crumbled away in the hands of their projectors, the goodly tree of British freedom, selecting from the kindly soil and assimilating its fit

never been a complete break in its continuity, and it can truly be said with Hearn in his *Government of England* that it is still the 'very constitution under which the Confessor ruled and which William swore to obey'. On the other hand, it has been subject to incessant modification in order to meet changing circumstances and changing ideas. No picture of it in any one generation is wholly true of it in another, any more than the picture of a man at some particular stage of his life can hold good for a later stage. That, indeed, must be my justification for attempting to portray the working of the Constitution as I see it to-day and in the light of the many changes which have taken place in the fifty years in which I have been in contact with parliamentary and public life.

At the same time our Constitution, throughout all the changes in its working, has retained its essential and original character. It is based on certain main features and inspired by certain vital principles which have remained constant and which have continued to assert, or reassert, themselves according to circumstances. It is not so much flexible as elastic, tending to revert to form as the influences which have deflected it in one direction or another have weakened or been superseded. It is to these main and vital features that I wish to draw your attention in this first lecture, because they may not only help to explain some of the changes of recent years, but also afford some guidance as to the nature of the even greater changes which may follow the political

nutriment, still increases its stately bulk and still extends its unequalled development. Outliving the storms and vicissitudes of centuries, deeply rooted in the habits and affections of the people, it spreads far and wide its hospitable shade.'—Hearn, *Government of England*.

and economic developments of the years immediately ahead of us.

There are, as Dicey points out in *The Law of the Constitution*, two main features from which all our constitutional development has proceeded. The one is 'the Rule or Supremacy of Law' and the other 'the omnipotence or undisputed supremacy throughout the whole country of the central Government'. The former feature was one deep-seated, not only in Saxon, but in all medieval thinking, until superseded elsewhere by the influence of Roman Law. The latter owes everything to the insight and masterful personality of William the Conqueror. With a clean slate to write upon he took care so to distribute the spoils of conquest among his followers as to prevent the building up of large territorial fiefs which might in course of time dispute the royal supremacy. In this way he laid the foundation of a strong centralized government which had no parallel in medieval Europe. In the long run, indeed, the clear gap thus created between the King and his subjects, great or small, tended to draw the latter together in resistance to arbitrary royal power and in defence of the recognized law and custom of the land. The barons and citizens who met together at Runnymede represent the obverse of William's policy when the royal power he created fell into tyrannous but weaker hands. At the same time William utilized the existing Saxon shire as a means of by-passing feudal authority through his sheriff, who, sitting in its court of freeholders as the King's representative and at the same time bringing the King's government in touch with local needs, foreshadowed the centralized parley between the Crown and the Commons or 'communities' of later days.

From William's day onwards the key to our constitutional evolution is to be found in the interaction between the Crown, i.e. the central governing, directing, and initiating element in the national life, and the nation in its various 'estates', i.e. classes and communities, as the guardian of its written and unwritten laws and customs. The ambitions or needs of the Crown continually demanded changes in the law which the nation was only prepared to accept after discussion or parley with its representatives and on terms. Out of that parley, progressively more continuous and more intimate as needs increased, and out of those terms, grew our system, as we know it, of Government in and with Parliament, subject to the ever increasing influence of public opinion and to periodic review by the nation as a whole.

The story of that evolution is so familiar to you that I need only touch on a few of its most salient features. The financial needs of the Crown long furnished the main lever by which Parliament increased its power. At the same time, the provision of actual money freed the Crown from dependence on feudal services and reinforced its effectively centralized authority. The same process of discussion and bargaining led to other changes or restatements of the law—at first suggested to the Crown by way of petitions, but from the fifteenth century onwards embodied in detailed Bills. These, whether initiated by or on behalf of the Crown or by Parliament itself, were then in their final form submitted to the King for his personal approval. No less important was the development by which the occasional parliamentary disapproval of the executive action of individual servants of the Crown, expressed in impeachment or attainder, grew into that milder but constant day-by-day questioning and criticism of Ministers with which we are familiar. Out of that development, helped by the doctrine that the King can do no wrong, sprang that division between the personal and the official powers of the Crown which is one of the most characteristic features of our Constitution.

The essential point to keep in mind is that in this process the Crown as an institution, in other words the element of government and direction, has maintained and, indeed, enormously increased the sum total of its power and influence. The Monarchy itself, divorced from arbitrary personal power, has become increasingly the symbol of the unity and continuity of our national and Imperial life. But that conception has not been without its profound psychological influence on the position of the Crown in its official capacity, both in the sense of responsibility which it infuses into Ministers and in the instinctive tendency of the nation to acquiesce loyally in their decisions, however open to criticism. That Ministers are His Majesty's servants does mean something both to themselves and to the public, however well known it may be that they, in fact, receive no orders from the Monarch in person, and that his power of dissenting from their conclusions on public affairs has shrunk by usage and sufferance to the narrowest of spheres. It is, indeed, customary to speak of that power as if it were limited in these days to a very occasional option in the choice of a Prime Minister among more or less equally eligible candidates. Of that I shall have something to say presently.

Meanwhile it is enough to say that in the present century the Monarch has carefully refrained from any such measure of intervention in matters of policy or

display of political partisanship or of personal objection
to appointments as Queen Victoria frequently exercised. But, within the limits of strict impartiality, the
King has more than once in recent years played a
mediating part in a political crisis, as for instance in
connexion with the Parliament Act of 1911, over Home
Rule in 1914, and again in the financial crisis of 1931.
It is believed, too, that the King's right to encourage as
well as to warn was not without its influence on the
settlement of the Irish question in 1921.

What is, however, important to keep in mind, from
the constitutional point of view, is that the Monarch's
personal power has never been abrogated or its precise
limits defined. Circumstances might conceivably arise
in which it might on some particular issue be reasserted
with national approval.[1] As to that it can only be said,
with Aristotle, ἐν τῇ αἰσθήσει ἡ κρίσις. The question can
only be decided in the light of all the circumstances of
the time, and the verdict of the nation alone will settle
whether such an assertion of the royal authority will
have been constitutional or not.[2] I would only add the

[1] The suggested hypothetical case of a House of Commons majority
using the Parliament Act in order to prolong its own existence for
partisan purposes was, in fact, met by a special amendment introduced
in the House of Lords.

[2] Constitutional authorities have argued that, in the event of such
action by the Monarch, any Minister subsequently accepting office
would, whether previously consulted or not, become ex post facto responsible. This is the view generally taken of the case of Peel in 1834, who,
by taking office after William IV's virtual dismissal of the Melbourne
Ministry, made himself responsible for the King's action. It would
similarly have resulted in 1936 if King Edward VIII had persisted in
his wish to broadcast against his Ministers' advice. It would then have
been for a new Prime Minister, unless assured of parliamentary approval,
to assume the responsibility of testing the judgement of the nation by
advising a dissolution. But such a strict logical deduction from the theory

obvious comment that such action, unless clearly of a quite exceptional character and confirmed by the judgement of the nation, might gravely affect the position of the Monarchy as the symbol of our national unity and as such above all party controversy.

All I wish to stress is that there is no absolute definition of the limits of that authority which can hold good for all time or for all circumstances. In the Dominions that authority, by usage somewhat wider than here, has in our time ceased to be exercised with reference to advice from a Secretary of State in London, and is exercised solely on the personal judgement and discretion of the Governor-General or Governor in his ultimate responsibility to the nation or State concerned. This was clearly established by Lord Byng's refusal in 1926 to consult me, as Dominions Secretary, when he decided to reject Mr. Mackenzie King's demand for a dissolution on the ground that the Leader of the Opposition in the Canadian House of Commons, Mr. Meighen, was able to carry on without one. In 1926 when an issue affecting the Governor's powers arose between Sir Dudley de Chair, then Governor of New South Wales, and the State Premier, Mr. Lang, the latter sent over his Attorney-General, Mr. McTiernan, in order to secure from me either assent to the principle that a Governor must always subscribe to his Minister's wishes or at least some definition of the limits of his rights to differ. With neither of these requests was I prepared to comply, basing myself on my statement in Parliament on 15 March 1926 that 'it would not be proper for the Secre-

that the King can only act on advice and can do no wrong seems more theoretical than real. In fact a new Minister would only be responsible for the situation as he then found it.

tary of State to issue instructions to the Governor with
regard to the exercise of his constitutional duties'. Sir
Philip Game, subsequently, in 1932, dismissed Mr.
Lang, basing his action on the latter's illegal conduct
in instructing State officials to prevent payments being
made under Commonwealth legislation whose validity
had been upheld by the High Court. The result of the
subsequent election confirmed the Governor's decision.

Still less capable of definition, of course, is the scope
of the personal influence of one who not only enjoys the
natural prestige of his position as Sovereign, but may
have the advantage of an even longer experience of the
inside of government than his Ministers, and who is
entitled to seek advice in every quarter, even if there is
only one source of advice which he is constitutionally
bound to follow. It has, indeed, been suggested that the
whole course of our constitutional evolution might have
been modified if Queen Victoria had continued to enjoy
for another generation the support of so able and far-
seeing a private counsellor as the Prince Consort.

To return to the main thread of my argument. I need
not go in detail into the well-known story, whether
strictly correct or apocryphal, of the origins of the
Cabinet as the outcome, in part, of Harley's informal
Saturday dinners, and, in part, of George I's reluctance
to attend Ministerial Councils at which, as he knew no
English and his Ministers no German, discussion had
to be confined to such Latin as they could muster
between them. The essential point is that the growth
of the system of collective responsibility, based on previous private discussion, strengthened the hands of the
Ministry not only as against the Monarch but also as
against Parliament. To single out an individual for

dismissal or denunciation is far easier than to denounce or urge the dismissal of a team, especially if the only alternative is another and even less welcome team.

Similarly, the most significant of all our constitutional innovations, whose beginnings go back to Walpole and reached their definite shape before the end of the eighteenth century, namely, the selection of a team of Ministers from among members of Parliament who could guarantee a working majority, while in one sense subordinating the policy of the Crown to party exigencies, yet, in another, meant an accession to the actual power of Government, as such, in exercising control over Parliament. It meant converting the leading poachers into the 'Crown's' gamekeepers. It meant converting the majority in Parliament into place-men, within at least the penumbra of office and influence, while at the same time under constant threat of losing their places (and nowadays their members' salaries) if their lack of support to the Government should cause the latter to dissolve Parliament.

At the same time neither Ministers nor their supporters have, in their individual capacity, ceased to remain representatives of the nation or of their individual constituencies. Nor have they entirely abandoned to the Opposition the original critical and debating function of Parliament. Subject to the varying strength of party discipline, government supporters can still criticize this or that feature of the Government's legislation or administration in public—and even more freely behind the scenes to the Whips or at party meetings in committee rooms. So, too, Ministers feel a kinship with other members, with whom they share the responsibilities and problems with which they have to deal in their constituencies.

What is more, they hope, even if they lose office, to remain in Parliament and so continue to exercise their influence over affairs pending their return to power. They are parliamentarians first and for the greater part of their public life; Ministers of the Crown at intervals. It is as parliamentarians that they are first tested and judged, both for ability and for character, by their seniors and their fellows, that they win and then keep or lose their right to office. Above all, whether Ministers or back-benchers, in office or in opposition, they are all subject to the firm and impartial control of Mr. Speaker, as the embodiment of the traditions of Parliament and of the rights of its humblest member. All these factors have combined to keep Parliament as the centre and focus of the nation's affairs, the conspicuous stage on which the great drama is acted, the great game of politics played. It is their interlocking and interchangeability which have maintained the unity and harmony of our political life, and it is in that sense that we rightly boast of our system as one of parliamentary government.

All the same, throughout the evolution of that system, the two main elements of our political life have remained distinct, though progressively harmonized and integrated. Our Constitution is still, at bottom, based on a continuous parley or conference in Parliament between the Crown, i.e. the Government as the directing and energizing element, and the representatives of the Nation whose assent and acquiescence are essential and are only to be secured by full discussion. The whole life of British politics, to quote Bagehot, 'is the action and reaction between the Ministry and the Parliament'. One might almost say to-day 'between the Ministry and the

Opposition', for it is the latter upon which has devolved most of the original critical function of Parliament.

Montesquieu was not, in fact, so wide of the mark as is sometimes thought when he made the division and equipoise of powers in our Constitution its chief characteristic and the secret of its success. It must be remembered that when he published his *Esprit des Lois* in 1748 the solution of ensuring stable majorities for the Crown in Parliament by entrusting office to those who could guarantee those majorities had not been fully explored. In any case he was contrasting the English give and take between independent and coequal political forces and the independence of our judges—the natural and logical consequence of our conception of the reign of law—with the rigid centralization of all power in the French Monarchy. To that extent he was only in line with Blackstone's dictum: 'herein consists the true excellence of the English government that all the parts of it form a natural check upon each other'.[1]

Where Montesquieu went astray was in treating the division as one between the executive and legislative functions, abstractions bearing no relation to the reality of our political life. Parliament is not, and never has been,

---

[1] So, too, Hearn argues that the classification of governments by external form, e.g. monarchical, oligarchic, democratic, gives no clue to their real character, and points out the danger to freedom involved in any system of government which places an undivided sovereignty in any one hand or set of hands: 'The distinctive character of a free or constitutional government is the composite character of its sovereignty and not the plurality of sovereigns. The distinctive character of Imperialism (i.e. Caesarism or dictatorship) is the unity of its power, not the individuality of the person in whom it is vested. . . . If the whole power of the State be centred in one body, if thought and speech and action depend upon the will of one person or one set of persons, that Government . . . is an absolute Government.'—*The Government of England*.

a legislature, in the sense of a body specially and primarily empowered to make laws. The function of legislation, while shared between 'King, Lords and Commons in Parliament assembled', has always been predominantly exercised by Government which, indeed, has never allowed Parliament as such to take any initiative in one of its most important fields, that of finance. The main task of Parliament is still what it was when first summoned, not to legislate or govern, but to secure full discussion and ventilation of all matters, legislative or administrative, as the condition of giving its assent to Bills, whether introduced by the Government or by private members, or its support to Ministers.

Montesquieu's error remains of interest, for on it the Fathers of the American Constitution based a constitutional structure which they believed reproduced the best features of the British Constitution. The practical inconveniences resulting from this artificial severance between functions which, in the nature of the case, are largely interdependent is an obvious weakness of the American Constitution. On the other hand, the President's freedom from the vagaries of parliamentary interference and his fixed tenure of office were, no doubt, in the past steadying factors in a young community continuously absorbing new elements with no common tradition. The Fathers of the American Constitution were, however, under no illusion as to one essential difference in the character of the two constitutions. Inspired in part by the republican tradition of the Puritans and even more by current individualist theories of the foundation of the State, they made the individual citizen the starting-point and motive power of the political process, the creator both of the President as the

embodiment of the citizen's executive authority and of
Congress as the embodiment of his power over legislation. On that issue they knew they were departing
directly from the British tradition. It may, indeed, be
said that for the underlying British conception of
balance and adjustment between two coequal elements,
each enjoying original and independent authority, they
substituted the citizen voter, or the numerical majority
of citizen voters, as the antecedent and ultimate source
of authority.

More serious in its consequences, not so much for ourselves, perhaps, as for other countries, was the misread-
ing of the essential nature of our Constitution in the last
century by writers of the dominant Liberal individualist
school, of whom Bagehot was the typical or, at least,
most popular exponent. Interpreting the parliamentary
situation of their own time in the light of their general
prepossessions, they persuaded themselves that our Constitution had, in fact, become what they thought it ought
to be, namely a system based on the delegation of
authority by the electorate to a Parliament which, in
its turn, delegated the day-by-day exercise of that power
to a Cabinet which was, in substance, only a committee
—to use Bagehot's phrase—of the parliamentary majority. That reinterpretation, though queried by eminent
authorities like Seeley and Lowell, and contested fundamentally by so thoughtful a constitutionalist as Hearn,
became the prevalent text-book theory, and still colours
most current journalistic and political phraseology.[1]

[1] How little real importance the writers of that period assigned to the
part played by the Crown, as embodied officially in the Cabinet, is indicated by the fact that not one of the eighteen chapters of Mill's *Representative Government* is devoted to the functions of the Cabinet. So stalwart
a survivor of the mid-Victorian Liberalism as my old chief Lord Courtney

There was, indeed, much in the external circum-stances of the time to encourage their assumptions. The mutual interlocking of Government and Parliament had by then been fully achieved. The *laissez-faire* theories of the age in economic matters and the absence of any serious external menace since Trafalgar and Waterloo had reduced the active work, both of administration and of legislation, to a minimum. A few broad issues of general policy could be spread over prolonged and elo-quent debates. Parliamentary debate as such domi-nated the attention of the public and created the great parliamentary figures of that day. In the comparatively evenly balanced and less strictly disciplined Parliament of the time, with both parties and the electorate itself drawn from a limited social stratum, it was not un-natural to conclude that Parliament, which so frequently upset Government, was in fact the body which governed and did so in response to the positive wishes of an actively interested electorate.

What was not foreseen by the Radical reformers of those days was that the progressive extension of the franchise, on the one hand, and the continuous increase in the volume of government work, on the other, would, by leading to stronger party organization in the country and to stricter party discipline in Parliament, reinforce the inherent tendency, in our system, for government,

---

of Penwith, in his *Working Constitution of the United Kingdom*, writing as late as 1901, could still dismiss the Cabinet in five pages out of nearly 200 devoted to Parliament, and could speak of the 'absolutely unqualified supremacy of Parliament' as 'embodying the supreme will of the State' to which 'every partial authority must yield'. In this respect the Socialist party has inherited many of the theoretical misconceptions of its Liberal precursors and Mr. Laski himself has referred to the executive as a 'Com-mittee of the Legislature'.

as such, to reassert itself whenever the opportunity or the need might arise. As for the fears of Conservative critics, whatever dangers or disadvantages may, or may not, have resulted from the spread of democracy in this country, the weakening of government has not been one of them. The strength of the innate tendency of our governmental tradition has been sufficient to overcome the danger which Burke foresaw in democracy, as preached by the individualist school, when he wrote:[1]

'No legislator has willingly placed the seat of active power in the hands of the multitude; because then it admits of no control, no regulation, no steady direction whatever. The people are the natural control on authority; but to exercise and to control together is contradictory and impossible.'

In that respect our Constitution has throughout conformed to that principle of balance between initiative and control which Burke laid down. It has never been one in which the active and originating element has been the voter, selecting a delegate to express his views in Parliament as well as, on his behalf, to select an administration conforming to those views. The starting-point and mainspring of action has always been the Government. It is the Prime Minister who, in the name of the Crown, makes appointments and confers honours without consulting Parliament. It is the Prime Minister, in the name of the Crown, who summons Parliament. It is the Government which settles the programme of parliamentary business and directs and drives Parliament in order to secure that programme. If Parliament fails to give sufficient support it is the Government, or

---

[1] *Appeal from the New to the Old Whigs.*

an alternative Government, which, in the name of the Crown, dissolves Parliament.

At a general election the voter is not in a position to choose either the kind of representative or the kind of government he would like if he had a free choice. There is a Government in being which he can confirm or else reject in favour of the alternative team. The candidates before him—the only candidates worth taking seriously —are either supporters of the team in office or of its rivals for office. It is within those narrow limits that his actual power is exercised. He may be influenced by the personality of the candidates, still more by that of the leaders of the parties, by a Government's record or by its opponents' promises, by sheer party loyalty or light-hearted desire for a change. No doubt, too, he has had his continuous share in the making of that public opinion which helps to shape parties and influence governments. But by the time it comes to an actual decision his function is the limited and essentially passive one of accepting one of two alternatives put before him.

Our whole political life, in fact, turns round the issue of government. The two-party system is often referred to as if it were the happy result of an accidental historical development, or as the consequence of a natural division between two types of mind.[1] Both statements contain a substantial element of truth. But the decisive and continuous influence has been the fact that a governing team with a majority in Parliament can normally only be displaced by another team capable of securing an

[1] The actual shape of the Chamber with its direct confrontation of the two Front Benches at close range helps to emphasize the continuous conflict between two sets of competitors for office. The case for its retention was eloquently stated by Mr. Churchill in the debate on the rebuilding of the House of Commons in January 1945.

alternative majority. Parties which are not in a position
to make their own government may, like the Labour
party in the early years of the century, represent the
intrusion of a new school of political thought, content
to make its voice heard and its influence felt, pending
the day when they can take office for themselves. Or,
like the Liberal party to-day, they may be survivals of
a past political alinement, not yet despairing of resuscita-
tion or at least of influence as a balancing factor. But
they are essentially transition phenomena. The two-
party system is the natural concomitant of a political
tradition in which government, as such, is the first consideration, and in which the views and preferences of
voters or of members of Parliament are continuously
limited to the simple alternative of 'for' or 'against'. It
is, indeed, only under the conditions created by such a
tradition that there can be any stability in a government dependent from day to day on the support of a
majority in Parliament.

It is precisely on that issue that the nineteenth-
century Liberal exponents of our constitutional system
so grievously misled the outside world. They created
the belief that it was possible successfully to combine the
British form of Constitution with the prevalent continental conception, derived from the French Revolution,[1]
of political power as a delegation from the individual

[1] Disraeli's phrase, 'the Anglo-Gallic scheme', shrewdly summarized
both the conception and the absurdity of its application to any and every
country, regardless of its traditions or social structure. 'If the barren
adoption of a form of government by France, styled by courtesy the
English Constitution, must be classed among the prime follies of human
conduct, what language are we to use when the Anglo-Gallic scheme
is gravely introduced to the consideration of the lazzaroni of Naples and
the hidalgos of Spain; we seem to have arrived at the climax of human
absurdity.'—*Vindication of the English Constitution*, ch. vii.

citizen through the legislature to an executive dependent on that legislature. That conception naturally involves the widest freedom in the citizen's choice of party regarded as the end in itself. In many countries it has led to the almost indefinite multiplication of parties.[1] Another consequence has been the adoption of systems of proportional representation, usually based on party lists, in order to secure for the individual voter or individual party their fair share of the composition of the legislature. It equally implies the right of the legislature to the initiative in all respects, including finance, and the denial to the Government of the power of dissolution. All these logical deductions have, indeed, been asserted as self-evident consequences of popular and parliamentary sovereignty by the great majority of those who have been engaged in drafting the new French Constitution.

Such a system of government, not in and with Parliament, but by Parliament, is bound, by its very nature, to be weak and unstable, subject to the continual shifting and reshuffling of coalition ministries and to the influence of personal ambitions. Face to face with the growing need of the age for more governmental action and more definite leadership, it has almost everywhere broken down. The rise of dictatorships and of one-party governments has been the almost inevitable consequence of the ineffectiveness of constitutions which reproduced the outward form of the British Constitution without that spirit of strong and stable government which is of its essence. The danger in Europe to-day is

---

[1] There were twelve parties in the Italian Parliament before the Fascist Revolution and, at one time, over thirty in Germany and in Czechoslovakia.

that we seem to be laying all our emphasis on urging the reproduction everywhere of those same externals, and asserting that same misinterpretation of the character of British 'democracy', instead of laying stress on the need for strong and stable government first and then leaving it to each country in the light of its particular conditions to find the way to reconciling that essential with public opinion and popular consent. We may thus be only too successful in paving the way for the spread of Communism or of some variant of Fascism that will offer what Europe most needs and what we seem unable to supply. Nor is the danger confined to Europe. All over the East and, not least, within our own Empire, we have created a demand for constitutional forms which can only work in a homogeneous community like ours and under a tradition in which all the emphasis lies on the strength and stability of government. We have never tried to think out alternative forms which could preserve the real character of our Constitution adapted to wholly different conditions.[1]

Democratic government based, in principle, at least, on delegation from below can, no doubt, be made to work. But in order to do so, the Government, however chosen, must enjoy a real measure of independence and for a reasonably long period. The United States affords one example. An even better example is Switzerland, where the executive is directly elected by the legislature

[1] The point is one made by Burke in his letter to a Member of the French National Assembly: 'When I praised the British Constitution and wished it to be well studied, I did not mean that its exterior form and positive arrangement should become a model for you or for any people servilely to copy. I meant to recommend the principles from which it has grown and the policy on which it has been progressively improved out of elements common to you and to us.'

and reflects its composition, but once elected, remains
independent for the lifetime of the legislature. In France
General de Gaulle, with a just insight into the weakness
of the existing French political outlook, has recently
proposed, in order to ensure continuity and as the only
safeguard against the danger of dictatorship, a blend of
the American and British systems in which executive
power and initiative are effectively centred in the President and the Ministry and not in the Chamber.[1] What
cannot work, as Mill[2] himself admitted, and as Crom-
well decided somewhat more forcibly before him, is
government by an elected assembly or subject to continual direct dictation and interference by such an
assembly. In any case that is not the kind of government under which we live ourselves. Our system is one

[1] 'Executive power cannot issue from the . . . Parliament exercising
legislative power without degenerating into a confusion of functions in
which the Government would in a short time be nothing but a collection
of delegations. . . . Executive power must therefore emanate from the
Head of the State, placed above parties and elected by the electoral
college which includes Parliament but is wider than Parliament. . . .
It is his function to name Ministers and above all to name the Prime
Minister who is called upon to direct the policy and work of the government. It is the function of the Head of the State . . . to preside at Cabinet
meetings and exercise there that influence of continuity which no nation
can do without. It is his function to serve as arbitrator above political
contingencies, either nominally through the Cabinet or in moments of
serious confusion, by inviting the country to express its sovereign
decision in elections.'—General de Gaulle, Bayeux, 16 June 1946.

[2] 'Instead of the function of governing, for which it is radically unfit,
the proper office of a representative assembly is to watch and control
the government: . . . To be at once the nation's Committee of Grievances
and its Congress of Opinions. . . . Nothing but the restriction of the
function of representative bodies within these rational limits, will enable
the benefits of popular control to be enjoyed in conjunction with the
no less important requisites (growing ever more important as human
affairs increase in scale and complexity) of skilled legislation and administration.'—J. S. Mill, Representative Government.

of democracy, but of democracy by consent and not by delegation, of government of the people, for the people, with, but not by, the people.

How far astray the prevalent mid-Victorian theory of our Constitution was from the reality even of that age, and still more so of ours, may be seen if we compare Bagehot's definition of the Cabinet as a committee of Parliament, or rather of the majority in Parliament, with the actual process by which Cabinets come into being and are, in fact, constituted. A committee usually implies definite appointment in detail by the parent body. Nothing of the sort takes place in the creation of a British Cabinet. The starting-point is the selection by the Monarch of a Prime Minister. The Monarch's choice, like that of the voter, may in most cases be very limited. If the majority party has a recognized leader, that is the obvious person to send for. Still there may be occasions when the Monarch's personal judgement can be exercised as between possible alternatives. The most recent case quoted by the text-books is that of Queen Victoria's selection of Lord Rosebery instead of Sir William Harcourt, whom the House of Commons would have preferred, or of Lord Spencer whom Mr. Gladstone would have recommended, if asked, in 1894.

There are, however, later instances. King George V's decision in 1923 to send for Mr. Baldwin instead of Lord Curzon (Mr. Bonar Law declining to make any recommendation) is often referred to as having been the natural consequence of the latter's being in the House of Lords and so under modern conditions disqualified As a matter of fact Lord Curzon's appointment was practically settled when two junior members of the Cabinet, the late Lord Bridgeman and myself, inter-

vened with Lord Stamfordham and urged reconsideration in favour of Mr. Baldwin as likely to be more
acceptable to his colleagues and to the rank and file of
the party. Lord Balfour, who was called up from the
country, agreed and suggested Lord Curzon's peerage
as a sound reason for passing him over.[1] The final
decision was, to the best of my belief, made mainly on
the issue of the personal acceptability of the two candidates. If a constitutional precedent was created, it was
largely as the *ex post facto* cover for a decision taken on
other grounds. Again, when Mr. MacDonald resigned
in 1931 it was the King's personal appeal to him and to
the Opposition leaders that kept him in office as the
head of a coalition, and that weighed with Mr. Baldwin
in not pressing his natural claim to be invited to form
a government.

Far wider is the field of choice open to a newly appointed Prime Minister. No doubt he has to consider
the claims and views of leading members of his party
in both Houses. But, subject to Parliament putting up
with his selection of his colleagues and his arrangement
of offices, he has a very free hand in shaping his government according to his own view of what is likely to work
best and according to his personal preferences. It is for
him to decide on the size of the Cabinet and what

---

[1] Lord Stamfordham in fact explained to Lord Curzon that 'since the
Labour Party constituted the official Opposition in the House of Commons and were unrepresented in the House of Lords the objections to
a Prime Minister in the Upper House were insuperable'.—*Life of Lord
Curzon*, i. 352.

So far as the merits of the question are concerned, the Duke of Wellington, as far back as 1839, expressed his own view that the Prime Minister
should be in the House of Commons, and so did Lord Rosebery after
his own experience of the difficulties of working with a Leader of the
House of Commons.

Ministers to include in it. He may consult a few leading colleagues or the Chief Whip or his personal cronies. In 1929 Mr. MacDonald settled his chief appointments in consultation with Messrs. Snowden, Clynes, Henderson, and Thomas. What formal or informal consultations may have taken place in the formation of the present Cabinet is not within my knowledge. Hitherto, in this country, at any rate, the Prime Minister has never been under any sort of direct dictation either from Parliament or from a Party Executive outside in making up his government. He may go outside the party ranks, or even outside Parliament, to choose someone whom he may think specially fitted for a particular post. Thus in 1903 Mr. Balfour offered the Colonial Office to Lord Milner, who was then still High Commissioner in South Africa and had never played any part in parliamentary life. In 1923 Mr. Baldwin offered the Chancellorship of the Exchequer to Mr. McKenna, a Liberal ex-Cabinet Minister, who declined on grounds of health, while Mr. MacDonald in 1924 made Lord Chelmsford, a non-party ex-Viceroy, First Lord of the Admiralty. Even more remarkable in its disregard of his party's views was Mr. Baldwin's appointment in that same year of Mr. Churchill to the Exchequer. At that time Mr. Churchill was almost the last person to whom Conservatives would have dreamt of entrusting that key position, not only because he had until only quite recently been a political opponent, but because he was known still to be vehemently opposed to the main constructive policy of the Party. But the appointment was made and the Conservative Party in Parliament, though never quite reconciled to it, grumbled and submitted.

Few dictators, indeed, enjoy such a measure of autocratic power as is enjoyed by a British Prime Minister while in process of making up his Cabinet. In France or in any other continental country which has imitated the outward form, but not the essentials, of our Constitution, newly appointed Prime Ministers have had to go round hat in hand to appeal for co-operation from political rivals each determined to make his own bargain as to the particular office he might wish to hold or as to the filling of other offices, and by no means sure that he might not do better for himself by holding back and waiting for the next ministerial reshuffle. With us there has been no instance of a Prime Minister failing to form a government owing to the irreconcilable claims or views of party colleagues since Russell's failure to form a government in 1845 because Grey would not serve with Palmerston. It was, indeed, widely bruited about in 1905 that Sir Henry Campbell-Bannerman could not form a workable government in face of the anticipated refusal of the Liberal Imperialist leaders, Asquith, Grey, and Haldane, to serve under him. But when it came to the point the strength of the Prime Minister's position easily asserted itself and they joined unconditionally. In 1916 Mr. Asquith resigned in the confident but, as the event proved, mistaken belief that, except for Mr. Bonar Law and Sir Edward Carson, no Conservative or Liberal of any standing would be willing to serve under Mr. Lloyd George.

A British Prime Minister may, no doubt, while forming his Cabinet, be besieged by insistent candidates for this or that office, but rarely is such a candidate prepared to reject the Prime Minister's final allocation. Refusal may mean exclusion from office, not merely for that Parliament, but for good and all. In 1924 Sir

Robert Horne, who had been a successful President of the Board of Trade and Chancellor of the Exchequer, refused the Ministry of Labour which Mr. Baldwin offered him. He was never considered for office again. It is only exceptionally forceful or fortunate political rogue elephants that, once extruded from the governing herd, can find their way back into it, as both Mr. Churchill and your present lecturer discovered for a decade after 1929.

This power of the Prime Minister to appoint, re-shuffle, or dismiss his colleagues continues throughout his term of office. It is, no doubt, mainly influenced by considerations of administrative or parliamentary success or failure. But it is a purely personal authority and makes the Prime Minister something very much more than a *primus inter pares* in the Cabinet. His exact position must always depend in large measure upon his own personality and that of his colleagues in the Cabinet, as well as upon parliamentary and party influences outside. But he is, in effect, both captain and man at the helm, enjoying, as undisputed working head of the State, a power far greater than that of the American President—so long as he does not actually forfeit the allegiance of naturally deferential and loyal colleagues in the Cabinet or of his followers in Parliament.

The fact that Parliament does not appoint but accepts a Prime Minister and a Cabinet is even more strikingly evident in time of war or acute crisis. Mr. Asquith's Coalition Cabinet of 1915 resulted immediately from Lord Fisher's resignation as First Sea Lord and from consequent negotiations with the Conservative leaders. It may, however, be said to have conformed to a general desire on the part of the House of Commons that he should strengthen his government by including the leaders of the Opposition. But the Lloyd George War Cabinet at the end of 1916 was not one that could have emerged from any method of ascertaining the wishes of Parliament beforehand. Few Liberals and still fewer Conservatives would have actually chosen Mr. Lloyd George as Prime Minister. Nor was there any demand, outside a very small circle, for a drastic change in the structure and working of the Cabinet as such. The whole affair was, in effect, a Palace Revolution brought about by a handful of men in the inner circle of the Asquith Government who were convinced that the war could not be won under the existing leadership and by the existing methods.

Still more notable, in that respect, was the formation of the MacDonald–Baldwin–Samuel Coalition of 1931. It is doubtful whether a Gallup poll taken in advance in favour of that particular solution would have secured even 10 per cent. support from either Socialists or Conservatives in Parliament. The bulk of the Socialist party, indeed, broke away as soon as it was formed, and the Conservatives only acquiesced on the most explicit assurances given by Mr. Baldwin to a party meeting that the emergency arrangement would be terminated the moment a balanced budget had been passed. By then, however, Ministers had begun to feel at home in their offices and to persuade themselves that the economic emergency still called for a 'National Government'. Unable to agree upon any policy to meet the emergency, they appealed to the country for a 'doctor's mandate'. The public, impressed by the vigour of the effort to balance the budget, and persuaded by a vast consensus of political and non-political 'expert' authority of the imminent danger of inflation and soaring prices, gave, by its vote, a majority in Parliament of ten to one, not so much for the Coalition, as against the unhappy and bewildered rump of the Socialist party. The subsequent necessity of having some sort of positive economic policy was met, for several months, by the fantastic expedient of certain Ministers dissociating themselves from the collective responsibility of the Cabinet and voting against its measures, and by their resignation after the Ottawa agreements.

The change of government in 1940 was, indeed, the direct result of a parliamentary demonstration of dissatisfaction with Mr. Neville Chamberlain's war leadership, and Mr. Chamberlain's recommendation to the King to send for Mr. Churchill coincided with the general feeling that the latter had the gifts which the occasion needed. As the basis of his government Mr. Churchill started with a more or less conventional inter-party coalition. But he freely enlarged and strengthened his administration by bringing in able outsiders to political life, fixing them up with seats in one or other House of Parliament as might be convenient.

I have purposely dwelt at some length on these particular instances in order to make it clear that, however essential it may be for a British government, once formed, to be sufficiently acceptable to Parliament to secure support in the division lobbies, its formation is in no sense the result of a parliamentary initiative and that its composition may bear little relation to the wishes and views of Parliament at the time. They are the result of an independent process beginning with the Monarch and carried on by the Prime Minister. It is still the Monarch who selects the individual who is likely to make the most effective Prime Minister and that individual who acts on his own responsible judgement of the situation. The Cabinet which he has formed then unite to support him to the best of their ability in administration and in debate, while those useful adjuncts to the Cabinet system, the Government Whips, fulfil their day-by-day duty of exhortation, encouragement, or discreet menace, in order to maintain the disciplined support of the back benches.[1] Government and Parliament, however closely intertwined and harmonized, are still separate and independent entities, fulfilling the two distinct functions of leadership, direction, and command, on the one hand, and of critical discussion and examination on the other. They start from separate historical origins, and each is perpetuated in accordance with its own methods and has its own continuity.

The continuity of government in our system is symbolized in the person of the Monarch. But it is also maintained in substance by the fact that the vast majority of the servants of the Crown carry on their duties permanently. What we call a change of government is, in fact, only a change in that small, if important, element which is required to direct the general policy, while securing for it parliamentary and public support or at least acquiescence. A change of government, to quote Hearn, means that:

'The vigour and uniform action of the Executive are maintained; but the direction of its forces is altered according to the wishes of the legislature . . . the vessel of state is entrusted to other hands and proceeds upon a different

[1] 'The Cabinet is an autocracy exerted with the utmost publicity, under a constant fire of criticism, and tempered by the force of public opinion, the risk of a vote of lack of confidence and the prospects of the next election.'—Lowell, *Government of England*.

course. But it is essential to the success of the operation both that the crew should be skilled in their work and that they should render due obedience to their commander for the time being, whoever he may be.'

The parallel, perhaps, suggests a much greater freedom than does in fact exist to change the ship's course— or, rather, the course of a fleet composed of a number of separate ships. Each of our great departments of State has its own tradition and policy, founded on long experience. Its crew has an accumulated knowledge of wind and weather, of reefs and shoals, by which a new captain is inevitably guided. It has its own private cargoes and destinations which a new captain soon tends to make his own and to advocate with vigour and conviction at the captains' conference. It may have projects for which the last captain could not secure that conference's assent and may return to the charge with better hope. In any case by far the greater part of the field of administration, and even of policy, is governed by factors which cannot be changed by party theories or prepossessions, or at any rate not to the extent which Ministers may have thought or said when in Opposition. The advent of a Socialist Government has not noticeably softened the heart of M. Molotov, or overcome the antagonisms of Hindu and Moslem in India or of Jew and Arab in Palestine. Housing raises the same issues of materials and man-power, of the relation of the central government to the local authorities, of the wishes of the people to be housed, whatever the political complexion of a government. The emphasis may be changed, new methods introduced. But much of whatever is done has to be a continuation of what was done before.

Our system of government is usually described as Parliamentary Responsible Government. It would be difficult to find a better description. But it must be remembered, first of all, that Parliamentary Government means government, not by Parliament, but to use the old phrase, government 'by the King in Parliament'. Secondly, that the responsibility is not merely one towards the majority in Parliament. Ministers on taking office accept a first and dominant responsibility to the Crown, as representing the unity and continuity of the life of the nation and of the Empire, for defending the wider national and Imperial interest. They accept, as I have pointed out just above, a corresponding individual responsibility towards the particular services over which they have been called to preside. As members of a Cabinet they accept, over and above their individual ministerial responsibility, a responsibility to and for their colleagues which is the basis of the collective responsibility of the Cabinet. As members of Parliament themselves they are responsible to Parliament as a whole and to the nation for the effective working of Parliament as the centre of our national life, for the maintenance of full and free discussion of every aspect of government policy, and for support of the Speaker in upholding the dignity and impartiality of debate. It is only subject to these wider responsibilities that, as party leaders, they owe a responsibility to their own party for promoting its particular views and forwarding its interests.

The word 'responsibility' has, however, two senses. It connotes not only accountability to an outside or final authority. It also connotes a state of mind, which weighs the consequences of action and then acts, irrespective, it may be, of the concurrence or approval of others. It is the strength of our constitutional system that it encourages and fosters responsibility in that higher sense. A British government is not merely responsible to those who have appointed it or keep it in office in the sense in which an agent is responsible to his principal. It is an independent body which on taking office assumes the responsibility of leading and directing Parliament and the nation in accordance with its own judgement and convictions. Members of Parliament are no mere delegates of their constituents, but, as Burke pointed out, representatives of the nation, responsible, in the last resort, to their own conscience.

Nor is the responsibility of the Opposition in these various respects any less than that of the Government and of its supporters. On the Opposition rests the main responsibility for what was once the critical function of Parliament as a whole, while at the same time it directs its criticisms with a view to convincing public opinion of its own fitness for office. It is with the importance of this responsibility in mind that Lowell in his *Government of England* said that:

'The expression "His Majesty's Opposition" . . . embodies the greatest contribution of the 19th century to the art of government, that of a party out of power which is recognised as perfectly loyal to the institutions of the State and ready to come into office without a shock to the political traditions of the nation.'

The same point was made by Lord Simon:[1]

'Our parliamentary system will work as long as the responsible people in different parties accept the view that

[1] In an address to the Empire Parliamentary Conference in 1937.

it is better that the other side should win than that the constitution should be broken.'

The combination of responsible leadership by government with responsible criticism in Parliament is the essence of our Constitution. Our aim must be to preserve it through the inevitable changes which the needs and demands of each generation bring about in its outward structure and in the adjustment of its parts.

II

HOW TO PRESERVE PARLIAMENTARY
GOVERNMENT

IN my first lecture I endeavoured to analyse the essential nature of our Constitution as one based on the balance and adjustment between two elements each of independent and original authority, the Crown and the Nation. The Crown, as represented by the Government of the day, is throughout the active, initiating, and governing element; the Nation, as the guardian of the laws and customs of England, is entitled to refuse its consent to any changes in these without good reason given. The arena in which the two conduct their continuous conference or parley is Parliament in which the Government of the day carries on its work of administration and legislation subject to the advice and criticism of the Nation's representatives. The struggle for predominance between the two which culminated in civil war was first adjusted by the compromises of the Restoration and of the Revolution of 1688, and eventually intimately harmonized by the device of the Monarch's selecting Ministers able to afford to the Crown the stable support of a parliamentary majority. This system is usually known as responsible government because under it Ministers owe a responsibility to Parliament and, in particular, to their own supporters in Parliament, in addition to their primary responsibility to the Crown as the embodiment of the unity and continuity of our national life. But I have suggested that it bears, or should bear, a wider meaning in virtue of the general sense of responsibility which it has engen-

dered in all concerned. Our all-important aim should
be to maintain that sense, as well as the place of Parliament as the centre and focus of our national political
life, throughout the profound changes which are inevitably affecting the work of government and of Parliament
and the fabric of our social and economic system.

The apparent predominance of Parliament over the
'Crown' which led mid-Victorian theorists to believe
that our Constitution had virtually become one of delegation from below was, as I have pointed out, the result
of an age when government was, in fact, reduced to a
minimum, leaving abundant room for spacious debating on a few broad issues of policy, followed with keen
interest by a limited electorate. It was an age in which
John Stuart Mill could with unquestioning assurance
describe the English people as having 'not the slightest
sympathy with the passion for governing . . . and there
are few things to which they have a greater aversion than
to the multiplication of public employment'.

The tremendous change in circumstances and in outlook which has since taken place has resulted from the
interaction of a variety of factors. The Industrial Revolution, with all its expansion of total wealth and power,
brought with it social consequences against which, even
in the hey-day of *laissez-faire*, the national conscience
revolted. Social reform, beginning with a mere trickle
of measures restricting the worst abuses of unregulated
capitalism, has in our century, under the stimulus of an
ever wider franchise, become a mighty spate of legislation aimed at securing at the public expense a reasonable standard of opportunity, security, and well-being
for the whole mass of the population from infancy to old
age. Each new measure has left in its wake a permanent

addition to that 'multiplication of public employment' which Mill believed to be so alien to our character, and ever fresh material for question and debate in Parliament—the sum total of all this accumulating at an almost geometrical rate of progression. The House of Commons, once the 'jealous guardian of the public purse', has less and less played that part, as its members came to owe their places to constituents of whom the majority think of themselves as recipients rather than as contributors—a process which, however, has nearly reached its limits.

External factors, meanwhile, have all the time been adding to the work of government both in actual administration and in Parliament. The increasing insecurity of the international situation over the last sixty years has led to the steady growth of the fighting services. Above all, two World Wars in rapid succession have accustomed the nation to regard the conscription of wealth and of man-power and even woman-power, over and above the drastic regulation of all economic activities, as normal things in times of crisis. The governmental machinery which enforced all these measures tends to be kept in being to deal with the many immediate problems of the post-war situation, as well as in view of far-reaching schemes of economic reorganization and in preparation for the possibility of even more terrible future conflicts.

All this has meant an immense increase in the legislative and administrative work of the Government and of its power over Parliament. Circumstances and public opinion alike have insisted that the work had to be done, and the leisurely amplitude of parliamentary discussion has had to suffer. When first I attended Parliament

as a member's private secretary fifty years ago the
House of Commons used to sit from early February to
the eve of grouse shooting in August. Only a grave
crisis could warrant such an unusual departure from
precedent as an autumn session. Autumn sessions began
to be increasingly frequent before the First World War
and have now become an invariable rule.

As for Private Members' Motions and Bills the time
allowed for these is of necessity being increasingly sacri-
ficed. Under existing standing orders, private members
have normally half Tuesday and the whole of Wednes-
day for Motions and the Friday half-day for Bills. But
the Friday was habitually annexed by the Government
after Easter even before the last war, and during the war
and since private members have had to forgo all their
normal rights and to be content with such very limited
opportunities as are afforded by the half-hour's daily
adjournment, 'prayers' for the amendment of statutory
orders and the motions for the holiday adjournments.
It has been said that the efforts of private members
rarely achieved any direct results, unless the Government was sufficiently interested to endorse them or to
find time for their later stages. But they afforded a useful opportunity for ventilating ideas and preparing the
public or the official mind for reforms not on the government programme. And one might quote not a few instances of important legislation directly introduced by
private members or resulting from their proposals. I
need only refer to Sir Cyril Entwistle's Matrimonial
Causes Bill of 1923, Sir Alan Herbert's Bill of 1937 on
the same subject, the Roman Catholic Relief Act of 1926
introduced under the 'Ten Minutes Rule' by Sir D.
Herbert (now Lord Hemingford), Miss Horsburgh's

Guardianship of Infants Bill, the Holidays with Pay Act of 1935, and the Population Statistics Act of 1938, not to speak of broader issues like female suffrage.[1]

[1] Since this lecture was delivered the Select Committee on Procedure has published its Third Report (189), including a very full and important memorandum by Sir Gilbert Campion, the Clerk of the House. The report brings out the fact that over the last forty years the proportion of parliamentary time devoted to legislation, administration, and finance has not varied substantially from a ratio of 50:40:10. But the volume of legislation has risen from 355 pages in the period 1906–13 to 642 for 1919–28 and to 995 for 1929–38. In other words, even before the advent of a Socialist Government the speed of legislation had increased nearly threefold. The more intimately legislation has touched our daily lives the less fully has it been discussed.

The report urges the restoration of the rights of private members, but suggests that instead of the allocation of time under the present Standing Order, private members should have the first twenty Fridays after the Debate on the Address, Bills and Motions being taken on alternate Fridays and balloted for as at present. It also recommends the restoration of the right of private members to introduce Bills under the 'Ten Minutes Rule'.

So far as Supply Days are concerned, the report recommends a simplification of the present procedure in favour of merging the present four days on first going into Committee of Supply as well as Supplementary Estimates with the other twenty days into a total of twenty-eight days. In order to avoid the undue restriction of debate resulting from the rule which forbids all reference to matters involving legislation, the report recommends that debate on the motion 'that Mr. Speaker do now leave the chair' should be excepted from the rule and that by mutual agreement between the parties this motion should be allowed on not more than four days additional to the first four on going into Committee of Supply.

The report also recommends the combination of the present Public Accounts Committee and the Select Committee on Estimates into a single Public Expenditure Committee, discussion of whose reports are to be given precedence on not more than two allotted Supply Days.

The Government have since (17 March 1947) announced their favourable disposition towards the proposals in regard to private members' time when that can be restored, and their acceptance of the suggestions with regard to Supply Days. But they propose to reduce these to 26 and to put no limitation on the number of occasions when debate may arise on the motion 'that Mr. Speaker do now leave the Chair'. They are

Even more serious has been the actual curtailing of debate on even the most important government measures. Second reading debates, once spread over weeks, are now rarely given more than a couple of days.[1] In Committee and on Report the closure and guillotine, originally introduced to cope with deliberate Irish obstruction, have been improved and refined by the over-all total allocation of time and by the power of selecting amendments left to the Chair.[2]

On the administrative side, issues of vital importance

opposed to the creation of a combined Public Expenditure Committee and regard an inquiry into delegated legislation as premature.

[1] The Government of Ireland Bill, 1893, took 14 parliamentary days for introduction and Second Reading, 28 days in Committee, and 3 on Report and Third Reading. The Education Act of 1902 took 4 days for Second Reading, 38 days in Committee, 6 for Report and Third Reading. The Parliament Bill, 1911, took 6 days for introduction and Second Reading, 13 days in Committee, 4 for Report and Third Reading. The Home Rule Bill of 1912 took 60 days in all. As against this one might set the following figures for important Bills passed in the present Parliament; National Health Service Bill, 3 days for Second and 1 for Third Reading; Coal Industry Nationalization Bill, Trade Disputes and Trade Union Bill, National Insurance Bill, 2 days each for Second Reading, 1 for Third Reading; Bank of England Bill, Civil Aviation Bill, Cable and Wireless Bill, one day each on Second and Third Readings. In all, 70 Bills, including 2 Finance Bills, were passed in the first session of this Parliament, a total actually outnumbered by the 102 Bills passed in the session 1919–20, but, in fact, representing a far greater legislative effort.

[2] This procedure, initiated in 1909, was formally embodied in a Standing Order of 1919 and has worked well, especially when, as in the case of the India Bill of 1935, Members have co-operated in agreeing upon the amendments to which they attach most importance. The fixed time-table has now been extended to Standing Committees. This the Government have proposed (17 March 1947) should be settled by a special committee. They also propose that the Chairman in Committee may disallow debate on the question 'that the Clause stand part of the Bill' if its principle has already been adequately discussed; also that the Report stages on the Budget Resolutions should be purely formal.

like international agreements tend to be brought before the House when everything is practically settled and a perfunctory debate has become only a concession to appearances. Thus a couple of days was assigned to the complete reversal both of Conservative and of Socialist economic policy involved in the acceptance of the American economic programme extorted as the price of the recent loan. Nor do the twenty supply days allotted to the Opposition really enable more than a few samples—and not always too well chosen samples—of the whole field of administration to be discussed.

These changes have had their effect not only upon the quality of debate but, even more, on public interest in Parliament. In earlier days any member who felt that he had a contribution to make to the subject under discussion could be reasonably certain of 'catching the Speaker's eye' at some stage of the debate. Careful preparation was well worth while. What was more, a reasonably good speech was certain of an adequate report in the Press, and the public followed with interest the progress of rising men or the utterances of those valuable authoritative members who, for one reason or another, are not candidates for office. To-day it seems to be thought obligatory for a government spokesman to open and wind up even a one-day's debate. With the same privilege accorded to the leaders of the official Opposition, to those of a minor party like the Liberals and even, to some extent, to fractional parties like the Independent Labour party,[1]

[1] In the case of the Liberals it may be said that the amount of time given them in debate, if disproportionate to their numbers in the House, does bear a better relation to their total voting strength in the country. But any group of members, however small, which claims to be a distinct

barely half, if that, of the total six hours or so of debate left is for those of the remaining six hundred who believe they have something to say. With only a problematical prospect of being called at all it requires a truly heroic devotion (or skill in subsequently converting an undelivered speech into a newspaper article) to prepare with any care.

In any case the back-bencher who is lucky enough to get in cannot expect to get more than a few sentences of his speech reported, probably those to which he himself attaches least importance. Not only is the range of subjects which the Press has to cover—and at this moment with a minimum allocation of paper—so much wider, but the subject-matter of debates is often too technical and detailed to interest the general reader. What really concerns him most is what the Government is going to do—for that may affect his pocket or his daily life immediately—and, possibly, what the Opposition leaders may have to say in reply. So the front bench speeches are still published more or less in full and the rest of the debate cut down out of all recognition, even by the most serious papers. The more popular or more whole-heartedly partisan press frankly distort the debate by magnifying trivial incidents or by suppressing the arguments of their opponents. The authority of Parliament has inevitably suffered in the process.

With these other changes has gone a great change in the composition of the House of Commons itself. The House of fifty years ago consisted almost entirely of

party, undoubtedly enjoys an advantage in this respect over larger groups within the main parties holding definite views on particular subjects.

frock-coated top-hatted men of substance, younger sons, landlords, big business men, leaders in the professions, none of them dependent on politics for a living, few of them able or willing to give their whole time to public work. It was, in fact, composed of the men who in the literal sense of the word owned and directed the country. Since then the House has been changed out of all recognition. In 1895 the House was nearly equally divided between the landowning class, big business, and the professions, the last mainly lawyers. In the present House professional men in the widest sense of the word form the main body of some 250, with some 170 manual workers or ex-manual workers as the second largest group, and with the balance, mostly in the Opposition ranks, divided between business and the old landowning and Services class. What, indeed, at one time was regarded as a revolutionary change, the admission of women to the House of Commons, and even to ministerial office, has, in fact, made very little appreciable difference to the actual character of the House, though the suffrage has undoubtedly increased the attention paid to issues affecting family life.

What is more, membership has become a very different occupation. Members to-day are expected to be at the House, not only all the afternoon and evening, but in ever increasing proportion for committee work in the morning. The 'best club in London' has become an overworked legislation factory, with a working day from 10.30 a.m. to 10.30 p.m. or later. Constituencies become ever more exacting in their claims on members' time during the recess and at week-ends. Politics are thus becoming more and more, for those who take them at all seriously, an all-time or most-of-the-time profession.

It is not a financially attractive profession for men of ability, even with the recent increase of payment to £1,000 a year. Its prizes, indeed, have lost enormously in real value while retaining their nominal amount. With present-day income tax and surtax and the far higher cost of living, a Cabinet Minister's £5,000 a year is barely worth a quarter of what it was even at the beginning of the century. The ordinary member's parliamentary income can, however, be fairly easily supplemented, or in the event of loss of seat, replaced, by other part-time and incidental occupations such as journalism, directorships, trade-union secretaryships, &c. Ministers, who have to give up all such sources of income on taking office, may, no doubt, often find no little difficulty in re-establishing them. The change, not only in the back benches, but even more, perhaps, in the ministerial ranks, is in many respects parallel to that which has taken place in the business world, where the old-fashioned capitalist who both owned and managed his works has been replaced by professional directors and works managers. We are, in fact, undergoing something like a 'managerial revolution' in politics.

The most important change, however, in the last half-century, and the most serious political menace to our whole system of parliamentary government, lies in the enormous development of the power of the party machine. 'Party', to quote Burke, 'is a body of men united for promoting by their joint endeavours the national interest upon some particular principle upon which they are all agreed.' It affords the natural means of organizing public opinion for the promotion of a new set of ideas striving to win acceptance, or for the defence of existing ideas whose permanent validity it wishes to uphold. By ensuring that the case for neither side is neglected it serves an important function in educating public opinion. In Parliament it gives stability and cohesion to the majority upon whose support any system of responsible government must rely, as well as to the minority whose responsible criticism is no less essential a part of the work of that institution. In the country it serves between elections to maintain contact between the public on the one hand and Parliament and Government on the other, and, at election times, to define and concentrate the issues. With us, as I pointed out in my last lecture, the two-party system has been the normal type to which, after occasional interludes, we have regularly reverted, for the very reason that it has always centred round the business of maintaining a majority in Parliament for a Government or securing its displacement by another Government. Our parties have been primarily parliamentary institutions looking for public support for their work in Parliament.

The progressive enlargement of the electorate[1] has involved an ever increasing need for political organization. Long departed are the days when it was thought sufficient for some local solicitor to see to it that the small percentage of the population qualified to vote were actually on the register, and when a rudimentary nucleus of party committees could be mobilized for action on the eve of an election. Whole-time profes-

---

[1] From 6,332,454 (including Ireland) in 1895 to 32,827,624 (including Northern Ireland only) at the present day.

sional agents work, year in year out, at keeping alive an elaborate network of committees in every constituency, not only to maintain enthusiasm but, above all, to build up a body of canvassers who, when the election comes, will sally forth to argue with the doubtful, but even more to persuade their sympathizers to take the trouble to walk or drive round to the neighbouring polling station. Above these are the district and regional organizers, and above these again the central office of the party with its head agent and its staff of interviewers, speakers, research workers, and propaganda writers. Parallel to this official structure there is also the more democratic structure of regional and national unions of constituency representatives, culminating in a national union or conference which meets periodically to voice its views and to come into direct contact with the leader of the party in Parliament.[1] All this is a natural, healthy, and, indeed, indispensable feature of modern political life.

The danger lies in the growth of the notion that such an organization, instead of being a useful and, indeed,

[1] The extent to which such a body should attempt to exercise influence and control upon the parliamentary leadership was the subject of no little controversy in the eighties between Lord Salisbury as Leader of the Conservative party and Lord Randolph Churchill as elected Chairman of the National Union of Conservative Associations. The same issue was raised by 'The Newcastle Programme' of the National Liberal Federation in 1891. In both cases a working compromise was arrived at which, in effect, retained the unfettered authority of the parliamentary leadership. In the case of the Socialist party the authority of the Party Conference, as well as of the Trade Union Congress, as bodies claiming a coequal right to influence policy at large, has been much greater. The party has retained an Executive separate from the Government, and even a Parliamentary Party Executive, though the strong ministerial representation in each of these bodies reduces the danger of irresponsible pressure on the Government.

indispensable adjunct to the work of the party system in Parliament, should in effect supersede it, directing government from outside Parliament and using Parliament merely as an instrument for carrying through policies shaped without reference to it. This danger of by-passing Parliament arises, not so much from party organization in itself, as from the same misconceptions as to the nature of our system of government and as to the meaning of majority rule which have wrecked the imitations of our Constitution in other countries. The first of these misconceptions is that our system of government is based on the initiative of the voter and on delegation from below. If that really were the case, then it would always be open to argue that the voter's party organization embodies his definite and final conclusions, his 'mandate', on all subjects and is, in fact, entitled on his behalf to prescribe the policy of the Government which he has created. Once that argument is accepted the party executive becomes the master and not the servant of the Government. Parliament becomes a mere instrument for registering its decrees. The personal character and quality of members no longer matters and debates lose all real significance. Policy is shaped, not in the light of full and free discussion, nor even in that contact with realities and with that sense of national responsibility and continuity which influences a Cabinet, but by an irresponsible partisan caucus, thinking only in terms of party aims or party interests. The danger of irresponsible power is even greater when an outside body, like the Trade Union Congress, primarily existing for industrial purposes, attempts to use its influence in party organization and finance in order to direct the general policy of a government.

The second and kindred misconception concerns the meaning of majority decision and majority rule. Decision by majority is not an absolute and unquestionable principle. Our Constitution, to use Burke's phrase, 'is something more than a problem in arithmetic'. There is no divine right of a mere numerical majority, of $x/2$ plus 1, any more than of kings. Majority decision is a measure of convenience essential to the dispatch of business, 'the result', to quote Burke again, 'of a very particular and special convention, confirmed by long habits of obedience'. Thanks to that convention Government is carried on with the acquiescence of the minority. When it comes to legislation it is of the very essence of our conception of the Reign of Law that it should not be regarded as a mere emanation of the will of the Government, but as something accepted by the nation as a whole. That requisite of consent for changing the law, or at least of acceptance when changed, is the root from which sprang our whole parliamentary system with its representation of the various interests and elements in the national life and with its elaborate provisions for full discussion. The idea that a majority, just because it is a majority, is entitled to pass without full discussion what legislation it pleases, regardless of the extent of the changes involved or of the intensity of the opposition to them—the idea, in fact, that majority edicts are the same things as laws—is wholly alien to the spirit of our Constitution.[1]

It is not unnatural, perhaps, that this doctrine of the

[1] 'Free Government is a day-to-day habit, a continuous political training in mutual respect and collaboration, in maximizing consent and minimizing coercion; it is not, as some simple democratic apologists think, a mere matter of legislative or administrative edicts backed by majorities' (D. W. Brogan, *The Free State*).

unqualified right of a party majority and the concomitant theory of ultimate control by a party executive
should in the past have exercised so strong a hold over
the Socialist party. Unlike the older historic parties
it originated outside Parliament, more concerned for
many years with organization in the country and with
dissemination of its principles than with the tasks of
government which, indeed, it has tended to conceive as
primarily, if not exclusively, concerned with translating
those principles into legislation. The Party Executive
was in its case anterior to any Cabinet or 'Shadow
Cabinet' and still maintains its separate existence and
authority. In Australia, indeed, Labour party executives
have insisted on settling in detail both appointments to,
and distribution of, offices in the Cabinet and have even
gone to the length of demanding from Ministers signed,
but undated, resignations enabling them to be recalled
at any moment.

Even here, as recently as 1933, Sir Stafford Cripps and
his co-authors in *Problems of a Socialist Government*
could advance the view that 'the Party' should appoint the Ministry subject to 'the right at any time to
substitute fresh Ministers in the place of any it desires
to recall'. Going even farther, they proposed that
an Emergency Powers Bill should be passed through
all its stages on the first day of the session, to be followed by an annual Planning and Finance Bill which
would 'take the place of the King's Speech, the Budget,
financial resolutions and the second reading debate on
most of the important measures of the year. . . . It is
idle once Parliament [*sic*] has decided upon a certain
course of action, to discuss its wisdom again and again.'
Freed from attendance at superfluous debates the

Socialist Members of Parliament were to be liberated as commissioners to see that 'the will of the Central Government is obeyed'. Mr. Attlee in setting forth the duties of these commissioners frankly accepted the comparison with the Soviet Commissars. 'We have to take the strong points of the Russian system and apply them to this country.' This would indeed, in Sir Stafford's words, have meant 'a complete severance with all traditional theories of government'.

Happily the passage of years, partnership in the conduct of a great war, and now the full responsibility of office would seem to have toned down these vagaries. The present Prime Minister and his Cabinet came into office in accordance with ordinary constitutional practice. They have pushed through their legislation expeditiously—some may think too expeditiously—but certainly on normal constitutional lines. There has been no violent breach of continuity in the great departments of State. Even the recent Party Conference at Bournemouth was marked by a domination of the debates by Ministers and a deference by delegates very much in accord with the tone of similar gatherings of the older parties. The traditions of our Constitution, like those of our parliamentary life, are, indeed, strong and pervasive, and tend to imprint their mould on even the most revolutionary elements. But it would be unwise to disregard the danger to the Constitution when widespread misconceptions of its character and spirit combine with the eager desire to reconstruct our whole social and economic life in the minimum of time through the machinery of an overworked and congested House of Commons.

There can be no setting back the hands of the clock.

Whether under Socialist or Conservative Ministries the sphere of government is bound to extend and with it the amount of business which Ministers must get through somehow in Parliament. What is required is a corresponding expansion of the capacity of Parliament to deal effectively with that business. If Parliament is to remain the centre and focus of our political life, both in fact and in public interest, and not to be by-passed in favour of secret party caucuses or public party or industrial conferences outside; if our Constitution is still to be based on a fair equipoise between Government and Parliament, in other words between leadership and criticism; then it becomes essential to bring Parliament into line with the magnitude of the tasks before it. The problem is one which has increasingly engaged the attention of those who have been occupied with public affairs, and many suggestions have been put forward for dealing with it. I propose to touch briefly on a few of the more important ones.

There are first of all those aimed at making better use of the time of the House of Commons by improvements in procedure and in the arrangement of business. The present Government has already felt obliged to withdraw almost all Bills, even the most important, from discussion in Committee of the whole House and to send them to the Standing Committees upstairs (now increased from five to six). Something is gained by this, but against the gain has to be set the loss from the sheer overworking of members. It should be possible to get rid of the technical necessity of a separate financial resolution for any measure requiring expenditure, which leads, in fact, not to a discussion of its finance, but only to a duplication of the main debate on its

principle. I have myself been inclined to wonder
sometimes whether time is not unnecessarily wasted, as
between the two Houses, in having all the stages com-
pleted in one House before it goes to the other, and
whether it might not be possible to bring forward the
second readings in both Houses, thus settling the main
issue of principle, before going into Committee stage.
This might even, without prejudice to the final authority
of the House of Commons, be dealt with by a joint
select committee of both Houses, coming back to each
House separately for the Report stage.[1] Nor can I see
any real reason why a measure which has passed through
some of its stages in one session should not be carried
over into the next session without, as at present,
requiring a special resolution, or even into a new
Parliament.

Far more controversial is the question of how far the
time of Parliament has been or should be saved by taking
the details of legislation out of its hands altogether and
leaving them to be dealt with under Orders in Council,
Provisional Orders or Regulations by Ministers—in
other words by civil servants. Much of our social and
economic legislation covers so vast and detailed a field
that no statute, however cumbrous—and many of them
are already cumbrous and unintelligible enough—
could possibly provide for all contingencies. Some
power of ministerial variation or interpretation is
obviously necessary, subject to the attention of Parliament being drawn to what is being done. In war the

[1] This can be done under existing procedure and was, in fact, done
with Lord Birkenhead's first draft in 1920 of the Law of Property Bill.
But it has so far only been done for additional inquiry and has not
dispensed with a separate Committee stage in each House.

need to give Government the widest powers to regulate the activities of its citizens and to provide for continually varying emergencies is such that parliamentary legislation can only provide the framework of principle and leave the detail to be covered by regulations.

But delegated legislation of this type has developed to an extent which has created serious apprehension. A Select Committee of the House of Commons was recently set up to examine these orders, rules, and regulations and, without discussing their merits, to call attention to those which seem to demand particular scrutiny. What is of particular importance in this connexion is to distinguish between the orders which should merely 'lie on the table' and those to which the special attention of the House should be directed by requiring positive confirmation. As the total number of these orders in 1942 reached the figure of 2,937, while 1,744 were issued in the eleven months ending last June, the Committee has found itself almost overwhelmed by the task. One member complained not long ago that the agenda for a single meeting weighed 1 lb. 7 oz.[1]

---

[1] In a third Special Report (186) published in October 1946 the Select Committee drew attention to the habit of sub-delegation of powers under the Emergency Powers (Defence) Act from (a) the Statute to (b) the Defence Regulations under the Statute to (c) the orders made under the Defence Regulations to (d) directions under the orders to (e) licences issued under the directions. They express the hope that now that hostilities have ceased departments may avoid this habit of cumulative delegation and be 'content with the grandchildren of the statute and not bring its great-grandchildren or great-great-grandchildren upon the scene'.

The Third Report of the Select Committee on Procedure (189) has since recommended that the whole question of delegated legislation should be investigated by a Joint Select Committee of both Houses of Parliament.

But it is not merely the spate of these regulations that gives cause for anxiety. It is even more the extent to which they tend to supersede law in the ordinary sense by ministerial edicts which, covered by statute, are not open to question by the Courts, or by ministerially appointed tribunals from which there is no appeal. There was an Act of Henry VIII's in 1539 which gave the force of law to the King's proclamations, and some provisions in recent Acts have gone very far in the direction of a reassertion of that principle. The whole question was examined by the Committee on Ministers' Powers which reported in 1932. It concluded that there was nothing radically wrong in the exercise of judicial or quasi-judicial powers by Ministers and of judicial powers by ministerial tribunals, but that the practice was capable of abuse and that certain safeguards were essential if the rule of law and the liberty of the subject were to be maintained. The subject is too technical for me to discuss the Committee's suggestions or the extent to which they have, in fact, been always complied with. But I might note that one serious constitutional anomaly, where the theory that the King can do no wrong has prevailed over the universal supremacy of the Law, namely the subject's inability to sue the Crown for damages for tort, to which the Report draws special attention, is still waiting to be rectified.

I come next to suggestions aiming indirectly rather than directly at saving the time of the House by improving the conduct of its business or the personal or representative quality of its members. One long-standing criticism of the work of the House is that its original and unique task of watching over expenditure is the least efficiently performed, if, indeed, it can be said to be performed at all. A committee which reported in 1918 on control over estimates pointed out that there had not been a single case in twenty-five years in which an estimate had been reduced on financial grounds, and that 'so far as the direct effective control of proposals for expenditure is concerned there would be no noticeable difference if estimates were never presented'. The twenty supply days of the session are, in fact, selected by the Opposition to raise issues of policy; rightly in my opinion, for policy comes first and governs expenditure. Nor is the House, as a body, capable of judging whether the actual execution of the policy which it approves is being economically conducted. Personally I doubt whether much can be achieved in this direction beyond the useful work already done by the Select Committee on Estimates. The real remedy seems to me to lie in the nature of the Estimates themselves and of our budget system as a whole and to come within the sphere of government itself.

More useful, to my mind, as a method of supplying the House with better information on many subjects than can be supplied by occasional debates and by questions, and of keeping Ministers more closely in touch with members on their special subjects, would be the institution of committees, either of the House of Commons or of both Houses, presided over by the Ministers concerned, of members interested in the work of individual departments. The objection has usually been made to this suggestion that similar committees in France or the United States have tended to be a great burden on the time of Ministers and, indeed, to have seriously impaired their responsibility. The objection, I think, overlooks the fact that the relation of Ministers to committees only reproduces in miniature their relation to the House as a whole, and that Ministers with us, unlike French or American Ministers, are unquestioned masters of the House and are supported in their position of authority by a solid majority there which is naturally reflected in the composition of its committees.

My own experience in the offices which I have held is that I should have gained by such regular opportunities of giving information and explaining my policies and of gathering the views of those interested, and that the effect upon the quality of debates would have been equally beneficial.[1] To some extent, indeed, the need for this type of contact has been increasingly met in recent years, and particularly in the present Parliament, by party groups or committees on departmental subjects. Liaison committees keep the work of these bodies in touch with the leadership of the parties. There are also the increasing weekly meetings of the parties as a whole. The drawback to this system is that Ministers may be too liable to one-sided pressure by their own supporters, while the Opposition Com-

[1] Lord Haldane's Machinery of Government Committee advocated such committees for their value not only to Ministers but to their departments: 'The particular argument in favour of some such system to which we feel justified in drawing attention is that if Parliament were furnished, through such Committees of its members, with fuller knowledge of the work of departments, and of the objects which Ministers have in view, the officers of the departments would be encouraged to lay more stress upon constructive work in administering the services entrusted to them for the benefit of the community than upon anticipating criticism which may be, and in present conditions often is, based upon imperfect knowledge of the facts or the principles at issue.'

mittees may miss some of the sense of responsibility which goes with official information.

You will not expect me to go in any detail into the much discussed question of Proportional Representation. Much of the argument in favour of a more exact representation of the views of individual voters, from the days of John Stuart Mill down to that indefatigable and persuasive champion of the cause in our time, the late Mr. J. H. Humphreys, is based on what I believe to be an erroneous conception of our Constitution. If ours is not an 'arithmetical constitution', and if the object of an election is not to ascertain an imaginary 'national will' or rather 'majority will', but to confirm a government that can carry on effectively in Parliament with national assent, then it is more important that a government should be returned with a working majority than that it should represent any particular numerical proportion of the electorate.

On the other hand, in so far as our system of representation is historically one, not so much of individual voters as of communities and of important elements in the national life, then there is certainly a case for seriously considering the application of Proportional Representation to our larger cities. These are now chopped up into arbitrary constituencies with no characteristic corporate life, while the numerical preponderance of the working class tends to deprive substantial and intrinsically important sections of the community of all representation. On the Continent the various forms of Proportional Representation there in use have both encouraged the multiplication of parties and strengthened the party machines. There is no reason to think that a similar result would follow here from a limited application of the single transferable vote, and it is at least arguable that stronger candidates would win and retain their seats than under the haphazard present distribution of constituencies within a city. An alternative method of strengthening the quality of the House would be to increase the representation of the universities and to add representatives from special professional organizations.

Every improvement in the quality of the House of Commons and in its dispatch of business would serve to revive public interest in its work and help it to sustain its essential function. But there is no reason why that interest should not be directly stimulated by providing better opportunities to the public for following its proceedings. I see no reason why more public money should not be spent in order to enable *Hansard* to be widely distributed as a penny daily paper or as an attractively got up weekly. But the real opportunity to my mind of rekindling interest in Parliament, or rather of creating it in a vast audience which takes in knowledge better by the ear than by the eye, and is increasingly accustomed to doing so, is to have Parliament broadcast on a special wave-length throughout the session. This has been done very successfully in New Zealand and Australia, where debates are being followed by the public with growing interest. I do not believe that this would lead to 'talking to the gallery' in the invidious sense of the phrase. On the contrary, broadcasting audiences are very critical of anything but sober good sense, and I believe the effect would be definitely to raise the standard of debates and to create an ever increasing body of parliamentary fans following the proceedings of what would become, not only the

Grand Inquest, but the Grand Brains Trust of the nation.[1]

Essential as it is to keep the House of Commons in the centre of the picture, I do not believe that any improvement in its procedure or in its composition will suffice to enable it to cope unaided with the volume of work that needs to be discussed or to provide the specialized knowledge required for the really useful discussion of the highly technical economic problems with which government will be increasingly occupied. Some substantial part at least of the work must be dealt with, or at any rate prepared, outside.

One most important contribution, indeed, to the problem has already been made in our time by the wide extension of local self-government. More than a hundred years ago Disraeli in his *Vindication of the English Constitution* was emphasizing the value of municipal government as a preparatory training in the parliamentary tradition and deploring the centralizing tendency of the Whig and radical reformers of his day. That tendency was reversed in the last quarter of the century by Joseph Chamberlain's work in Birmingham, by the setting up of County Councils in 1885 and of the London County Council in 1900, by the Education Act of 1902, and the creation of Territorial Associations in 1907, all marking stages in the building up of a vigorous local life which has both created a widespread, if still inadequate, interest in public affairs, and trained a great body of voluntary workers as well as its own professional civil service.

The question is how far the principle of devolution

---

[1] 'Without publicity there can be no public spirit, and without public spirit every nation must decay.'—Disraeli.

can be extended and how far it can in that case lighten
the excessive burden on Parliament itself. The successful working of provincial devolution in Northern Ireland suggests that there might be scope in the rest of the
United Kingdom for what Mr. Churchill once advocated as the restoration of the Heptarchy, viz. devolution to Scotland and Wales, and to large provincial
units in England. The powers assigned, to the English
provinces at any rate, might not be as wide as those
enjoyed in Northern Ireland. There would be obvious
difficulties in transferring Commerce and Labour for
instance. But in agriculture, health, housing, education,
poor relief, and local government generally, provincial
interest and inter-provincial emulation might well be
more important than uniformity. This devolution
need not, of course, exclude retention of concurrent
powers by Parliament, as provided in the Constitution
of Canada and under the India Act of 1935. It might
even provide for provincial legislation being 'laid on the
table' of the House of Commons for consideration.[1]

All the same, such is the magnitude of the tasks in the

[1] Federal Home Rule all round was Mr. Joseph Chamberlain's
alternative to conceding Home Rule on Nationalist lines in 1886, but
faded out of the picture as constructive alternatives often do. In June
1919 the House of Commons passed a resolution in favour of the creation
of subordinate legislatures within the United Kingdom and invited the
Government, without prejudice to the Irish question, to appoint a parliamentary body to consider and report upon a measure of Federal Devolution applicable to England, Scotland, and Ireland, with a somewhat
vague reference to Wales. A Committee of sixteen peers and sixteen
members of the House of Commons under Mr. Speaker Lowther reported in April 1920. The Committee were agreed in treating England,
Scotland, and Wales as units, but divided between those who favoured
a true federal solution with separately elected legislatures and those who
were not prepared to go beyond national Grand Councils composed of
existing representatives in Parliament of the areas concerned. The
Government took no interest in the matter, and nothing more happened.

national, Imperial, and international fields which only Parliament can handle that it seems necessary to envisage an actual expansion of Parliament itself both to fulfil its wider functions in general legislation and policy and more particularly to provide a more fully informed discussion of the ever increasing work of legislation and supervision in the economic field. The first and most obvious line of approach is to make better use of the House of Lords. This can only be done as the result of that far-reaching change in its composition which was promised in the Preamble of the Parliament Act of 1911, but has never since been seriously taken in hand. A distinguished Conference of members of both Houses under Lord Bryce reported in 1918 in favour of a Second Chamber consisting as to 246 members elected by the House of Commons divided into geographical panels and as to another 81 chosen by a Joint Committee in the first instance from the existing House of Lords. Mr. Lloyd George's Government repeatedly declared their intention of dealing with the matter, but did not get beyond moving some vague resolutions in 1921. Somewhat similar proposals, sponsored by Lord Cave, were put forward by Mr. Baldwin's Government in 1925, but hastily dropped at the first signs of adverse criticism.

My own conviction is that we shall do well to dismiss from our minds all elaborate schemes based on direct or indirect election,[1] and go back to the original character of the Upper House as a body whose members

[1] Disraeli, in his *Vindication*, long ago stated the objections to a reform based on some alternative method of election in the following terms, to my mind even more applicable to our present-day conditions: 'I cannot understand how an efficient senate is to be secured by merely instituting another elective chamber, the members of which being the deputies of their constituents, must either be the echo of the Lower

were specially summoned for the value or weight of the advice they could give to the Crown as individuals either in virtue of their territorial or ecclesiastical authority or on purely personal grounds. The habit of hereditary summons was a natural consequence of the inheritance of the estates which were the basis of local authority. Its development into a principle, irrespective of the function performed, was due to the lawyers. It was, in a sense, an approximation to the continental theory of a nobility of blood, though confined to actual heirs and not claiming even for these any departure from that equality of civil rights which Disraeli emphasized as one of the vital features of our Constitution. So long as the great landowning class played the part which they did in our social and economic life even a hundred years ago, and so long as they were not too unequally divided in their party complexion, the unreformed House of Lords could still justifiably claim a large share in the Constitution. The limitation imposed by the Parliament Act upon their powers of holding up the legislative activity of government was the almost inevitable consequence of political and social developments to which the composition of the House had failed to respond.

To-day the personal prestige and influence of individual peers, whether such by inheritance or by new creation, still stands high. But it cannot be said that the hereditary peerage, as such, is a body of sufficient real significance in the national life to warrant its constituting a House of Parliament in itself. The House of Lords to-day retains only one really distinctive feature, the

House, or, if returned by a different class, the delegates of an envious and hostile section of the community.'

individual independence of its members. The greater
the danger of the House of Commons increasingly consisting of representatives subservient to their electors or
to the party machine, the more essential is it that the
House of Lords should be representative in the wider
sense of embodying the typical characteristics of the
nation, its individuality, its independence, its broad
tolerance and love of compromise.

The only immediate reform I would introduce would
be the re-establishment of the principle of the life peerage. The suggestion is not a new one. As far back as
1857 the Government of the day attempted in the
Wensleydale case to create a life peer, but desisted,
without testing its legal right to do so, in face of opposition in the House itself. The case for life peerages was
effectively stated by the late Lord Salisbury in the
debate on Lord Russell's Bill in 1869:

'We belong too much to one class, and the consequence is
that with respect to a large number of questions we are all
too much of one mind. Now, that is a fact which appears to
me to be injurious to the character of the House as a political
assembly in two ways. The House of Lords, though not an
elective, is strictly a representative assembly, and it does, in
point of fact, represent very large classes in the country.
But if you wish this representation to be effective, you must
take care that it is sufficiently wide. . . . We want, if possible,
more representatives of diverse views and more antagonism.
. . . There are a vast number of social questions deeply
interesting to the people of this country, especially questions
having reference to the health and moral condition of the
people—and on which many members of your Lordships'
House are capable of throwing great light—and yet these
subjects are not closely investigated here because the fighting
power is wanting and the debates cannot be sustained.'

I would use the new power freely, but I would allow a reasonable number of years to pass, in order to enable the proportion of life peers to become substantial, and, even more important, in order to carry forward the tradition of the old House into the new, before proceeding to confine membership mainly, or even exclusively, to those summoned in person as Lords of Parliament. Even that change would not, in fact, be very marked. For I believe that the tradition of public service in the hereditary peerage is such that a very large proportion of its members would make it their aim to justify their titles by qualifying for their summons. The eventual limitation of the total numbers of the House of Lords would be a natural consequence of the Parliament Act, which has obviously superseded the need for so dubious an emergency expedient as the creation of peers to force through legislation.

The qualification for selection to the Upper House should be a wide one, based on every kind of public service or distinction, whether in Parliament, in local government, in the administrative or fighting services of the Empire, in business, trade-union organization, science, literature, or art. In the selection itself the Government of the day should have, at any rate, a dominating voice. But there are great disadvantages, as the experience of Canada has shown, in a system by which the Upper House tends to contain the maximum of supporters of one party at the end of that party's tenure of office, especially if it has been a long one, and is therefore most inclined to be at issue with a new government. This objection would be met if a proportion of the names were suggested by the Leader of the Opposition, possibly as a member of a small committee

of inquiry and recommendation under the chairman-
ship of the Speaker.

The restoration of life peerages would, of course,
greatly widen the field of choice by including many
poorer men or men to whose sons a peerage would
simply be an embarrassment. But it would only gradually reduce the disproportion of parties, at any rate on
the present party alinement. That is a disadvantage I
should accept for the sake of continuity. It would be a
mistake to destroy the essential character of the House
of Lords in order to meet the theoretical requirements
of a situation which may well prove purely transitory.
A party based on class, such as the Socialist party has
in the main been hitherto, is an anomaly due to our
failure to meet the economic consequences of the *laissez-
faire* period. Our object must be so to deal with our
economic problems that the future division between
our parties will be based, not on class interests, but on
differences of political principle with regard to which
the Upper House would then soon find itself more
evenly divided. That it should have a certain prepos-
session against violent changes is, indeed, inherent in
the function of any Second Chamber.

The existing House of Lords, while wisely refraining
from challenging the policies of the present Government, has undoubtedly been of real assistance to that
Government in improving its measures in minor detail.
A reformed House could not only deal more effectively
with supplementary legislative work of that character,
but on many subjects its initiative might largely make
up for the reduced opportunities of the private member in the House of Commons, while its debates would
carry increasing weight on broad issues of national and

Imperial policy. But it would not meet the most urgent need of our time, namely the fully informed discussion of the detailed measures required to carry out the increasingly complex tasks of our social and industrial legislation and administration.

It must be remembered that the growth of the party machine, on the one hand, and the change in the structure of our national life on the other, have deprived the House of Commons of much of its representative character. Our geographical basis of representation was originally also a real functional basis. The knights of the shire represented agriculture and, in the Middle Ages, more particularly wool; the burgesses represented a variety of localized industrial and commercial interests. Long after that, whatever party might win the election, the main elements and functions of our national life were represented in Parliament in proportion to their importance in the simple economic and political structure of the day. When the original scheme ceased to be even approximately representative more than a century ago, because it excluded great new industries and vigorous and politically conscious elements of society, it was still possible to meet the practical needs for a better functional representation by the suppression of the rotten boroughs, by redistribution, and by successive extensions of the franchise, without altering the geographical basis.

To-day, with the immense increase and spread of our population, with universal suffrage, and with the diffusion of industry and commerce, our geographico-arithmetical constituencies have to a large extent, for economic purposes at least, lost their justification as the basis of a representative system. The real units, the great collective elements of the national life, the industries that are its organs, are unrepresented except by accident or in the most one-sided fashion. Agriculture has been predominantly represented by landlords; coal-mining, on the other hand, almost exclusively by miners; engineering, building, transport, the distributive trades, science, and medicine only in so far as someone with knowledge of these matters has happened also, for other reasons, to be a member of Parliament.

The time has come, I believe, for a new and far-reaching Reform Act which will recognize the ever growing economic organization of the national life as a necessary basis of representation. The conception of the 'corporative' or 'functional' basis of representation has, indeed, already been, not only widely advocated in other countries, but to some extent tried out. The German Federal Economic Council established in 1920 would seem, for a time at least, to have enlisted the zealous co-operation of the best elements on both sides of industry and to have been regarded as a valuable coadjutor by the Cabinet and by the Reichstag in the field both of investigation into facts and of preliminary work on social and commercial legislation,[1] but to have fallen into the background in the economic and political confusion of subsequent years. The corporative system established by Mussolini inevitably suffered from subordination to the exigencies of totalitarian dictatorship and from its artificially devised structure. But the impression I derived from some study of its working in the immediately pre-war period was that, apart from a good deal of eyewash, it had in fact achieved useful

---

[1] See Finer, *Representative Government and A Parliament of Industry*, for the origins and initiation of this body.

results which might still merit investigation. Portugal has a *Camera Corporativa* or functional assembly sitting parallel with a Chamber based on geographical representation. In France the creation of a separate functional advisory Chamber seems to be one of the few generally agreed features of the new Constitution.

This conception of functional representation has, however, its own independent history in this country.[1] It was the recognition in the debate on the Address in February 1919 of the need for utilizing the wealth of practical knowledge and creative suggestion embodied in our industrial organizations which led to the National Industrial Conference and to the project of a permanent National Industrial Council of four hundred members, representative in equal numbers of employers' organizations and trade unions, which was recommended in April 1919 by a Provisional Joint Committee. That project was dropped in the general reaction against all creative reconstruction which followed the economic depression at the end of 1920. In that same year Sidney and Beatrice Webb published their *Constitution for a Socialist Commonwealth of Great Britain*, a most suggestive work in which the difficulties and dangers of attempting to carry out a great programme of nationalization with the existing machinery of government are searchingly analysed. Their conclusion, indeed, was the setting up of two entirely separate and co-equal Parliaments, a Political Parliament with collective Cabinet responsibility dealing with external affairs, defence, and justice, and a Social Parliament, working largely through committees and elected for a fixed period.

[1] There was, indeed, some talk of creating corporative constituencies at the time of the Reform Act of 1831.

More modest and more practical was Mr. Churchill's advocacy in his 1930 Romanes lecture of a House of Industry empowered, in a preparatory and advisory capacity, to deal with social and industrial problems. Such a body might embody its conclusions in resolutions or in draft bills for consideration by the Government. But it might possibly be worth considering whether the principle embodied in the Church of England Assembly (Powers) Act of 1919 might not be applied to such a House of Industry or National Industrial Assembly, or even to associations set up by individual industries or professions. Under that Act the Church Assembly has the power to frame measures, which may amend or repeal existing Acts of Parliament, subject to acceptance or rejection, as they stand, by Parliament. Many hundred useful measures have, in fact, been accepted, though public interest has only been drawn to the rejection of the two measures dealing with the revision of the Prayer Book.

The advantage of setting up a separate 'House of Industry' or 'sub-Parliament' is that the new principle of functional representation can in this way be tried, without destroying the existing geographical principle, which has its value, not only on historical grounds, but as the instrument, through the party system, of general national policy. The new Chamber would be one in which the great economic problems of the day could secure practical and responsible discussion, free from abstract party catchwords and programmes as well as from purely partisan manoeuvring for power. While the producers' point of view would naturally, and properly, be strongly represented, it is worth while keeping in mind that in such an assembly the majority would be consumers in relation to the claims of any particular group of producers. In any case the consuming interest could be strengthened by the addition of representatives nominated by the Government.

Such a body would, I believe, soon attract the best elements on both sides in industry, which would be willing to find the time for practical and congenial business which they will not give to the House of Commons under present conditions. It would, in particular, give a new and valuable scope to the activities and responsibilities of the trade-union movement and of employers' associations in their own appropriate field. Linked in this way with the actual control of the laws that governed them, both employers and employed generally would tend to acquire a more national point of view; to regard industry as a constituent element in the national life, directly contributing to, as well as dependent upon, the strength and health of the whole, and not merely as a collective phrase for a number of competing firms, on the one hand, and of workmen marshalled against them, on the other, each only concerned with immediate results in profits or wages.

In any case, the scope of the new Chamber would be definitely limited, and there could be no question of its attempting to compete with the House of Commons in the field of finance, of general legislation, or of administration. The House of Commons would still remain the central and predominant element in the parliamentary system, the point of junction between the Government and a politically organized nation, the pivot of our system of responsible government. The proposal for setting up a third House of Parliament may sound revolutionary. But it has after all the same warrant as the creation of the Air Force alongside of the older fighting services, namely, the emergence of modern conditions. And, just as the addition of a third Fighting Service has paved the way towards a more unified outlook on strategy as a whole, so it may well be that three Houses may combine to create a much more efficient and smoother working parliamentary machine than we have known in the past.

The essential correlative, however, of a more efficient Parliament is greater efficiency in the work of government itself. Parliamentary time is wasted, in the long run, quite as much by lack of foresight and clearly conceived policy on the part of governments as by defects in the procedure and structure of Parliament itself. Nor, indeed, are we likely to go far in the improvement of our parliamentary system until we have a government that is capable of devising a clearly conceived plan of reform, and has the determination to carry it through. It is to that aspect of the problem of the Constitution, namely, to the actual working of the machinery of government, that my next lecture will be devoted.

III

THE MACHINERY OF GOVERNMENT

THE central directing instrument of government, in legislation as well as in administration, is the Cabinet. It is in Cabinet that administrative action is co-ordinated and that legislative proposals are sanctioned. It is the Cabinet which controls Parliament and governs the country. In no other country is there such a concentration of power and such a capacity for decisive action as that possessed by a British Cabinet, provided always that it enjoys the support of a majority in the House of Commons. If that power is not always effectively exercised or directed by sufficient forethought the weakness lies, not in the constitutional position of the Cabinet itself, but in those defects of its internal organization upon which I propose to touch later on.

The essence of our Cabinet system is the collective responsibility of its members. All major decisions of policy are, or are supposed to be, those of the Cabinet as a whole. They are supported by speech and vote by all its members, and, indeed, by all the members of the Government in the wider sense of the word. The rejection or condemnation by Parliament of the action taken upon them affects the Cabinet as a whole, and is followed, if the issue is one of sufficient importance, by its resignation. The secrecy of Cabinet proceedings, originally based on the Privy Counsellor's oath and antecedent to collective responsibility, is in any case the natural correlative of that collective responsibility. It would obviously be impossible for Ministers to make an effective defence in public of decisions with which it was known that they had disagreed in the course of Cabinet discussion. There is no other mystery about it.

The collective responsibility of Ministers in no way derogates from their individual responsibility. If the two conflict a Minister may always resign or be requested to resign. In 1917 Sir Austen Chamberlain, as Secretary of State for India, resigned after the report of a judicial inquiry into the conduct of the Mesopotamian campaign for which he was technically responsible. In 1922 Mr. Montagu had to resign for publishing, without consulting the Cabinet, a telegram from the Government of India pressing for a revision of the Sèvres Treaty with Turkey. In 1935 Sir Samuel Hoare (Lord Templewood) resigned when the Cabinet threw over the Hoare–Laval compromise over Abyssinia. In 1938 Mr. Eden resigned in order to dissociate himself from the policy of conciliating Mussolini which Mr. Chamberlain was pursuing. The point has derived added importance since the innovation of War Cabinets excluding the holders of many of the most important offices. The responsibility of Ministers of 'Cabinet rank' for the general policy of the Government may have been reduced, but their responsibility for decisions relating to their own department is not affected or superseded by any over-riding responsibility on the part of the actual Cabinet.

The Cabinet normally consists of members of the same party, relying on the support of a disciplined majority in the House of Commons. This is the natural concomitant of our system of organized, and in a sense forensic, debates in Parliament and in the country on behalf of or against one or other of two alternative governments. But in times of national emergency only a Coalition Ministry can concentrate the mind, as well as the individual ability, of Parliament on the common task. So long as the emergency dominates everything such coalitions remain effective. They speedily acquire a corporate sense of mutual loyalty and goodwill, and such divisions as occur tend to be much more the outcome of differences of temperament and individual outlook than of party affiliation. They may even afford incidental opportunity for far-reaching agreed reforms such as the franchise reforms and Mr. Fisher's Education Act of the Lloyd George War Cabinet or Mr. Butler's recent Education Act and that whole recasting of our social security system, usually associated with the name of Lord Beveridge, which was framed and partly carried out under Mr. Churchill.

On the other hand, outside the immediate action required to deal with a supreme emergency, they lack the underlying unity of outlook and similarity of instinctive reaction of a party Cabinet and are even more prone to hand-to-mouth decisions based on no consistent policy. On issues where there is a fundamental divergence there is a tendency to evade discussion or, if postponement is impossible, to find weak compromises defended on grounds which shirk the real issue of policy. It was the inconsecutiveness, no doubt in part due to the Prime Minister's own temperament, of the Lloyd George post-war coalition that irritated the Conservative Party into eventual revolt. The MacDonald–Baldwin Coalition petered out through the successive stages of Ministers' 'freedom to differ' on the main policy of the Government and of subsequent resignations, into a Conservative Government of a somewhat nondescript type.

The 'Keystone of the Cabinet Arch', to quote Lord Morley, is the Prime Minister, with powers always great and in an emergency 'not inferior to those of a dictator'. It is his Cabinet and he has in large measure created it; he can at any time change its composition; his is the decisive voice in bringing it to an end by dissolution or resignation.[1] He decides when it is to be convened and what it is then to discuss. He equally sums up the result of the discussion after duly considering the arguments and the personal weight of those who have used them. He may, on occasion, take a vote, but this is the exception, at any rate on issues of major importance. I have never myself known a vote asked for by another member of the Cabinet.

For the rest, all is a matter of the Prime Minister's personality and that of his colleagues. Some Prime Ministers have been little more than chairmen of a committee concerned only with securing the greatest possible measure of agreement between more forceful colleagues. Others have been determined to get their own way, it might be by directly dominating the situation at the Cabinet, or it might be as the result of quiet talks outside with those whose opinions carried most weight. Some have been businesslike, have read all the papers up for discussion, and been mainly concerned to get decisions. Some have believed

[1] As regards a Prime Minister's position in regard to a dissolution, Lord Oxford and Asquith, in his *Fifty Years of Parliament*, stated that such a question 'is always submitted to the Cabinet for ultimate decision'. That does not seem to have been the case since the First World War. Mr. Baldwin did not consult the Cabinet formally before speaking to the King in 1923 or 1935. Nor did Mr. Churchill do so in 1945. The matter may well be one which in these days of formal agenda and records a Prime Minister may consider more suitable for informal discussion with leading colleagues and party organizers outside the Cabinet room.

in letting everybody ventilate their troubles and in the value of desultory conversation. Some have been natural listeners disposed to lie low and say nothing, either waiting to see what others thought or in order to come in with their own decisive intervention to conclude the debate. Others have been inclined towards government by monologue. Some have tended to be wet blankets and some have been an inspiration. Some have made a point of seeing something of all their colleagues, and even of junior Ministers, individually. Some have mainly confined their talks to an informal 'inner Cabinet'. Others have seen little of their colleagues except at Cabinet meetings. Some Cabinets have been happy families, others have not.

It was, until quite recently, generally supposed that Cabinet meetings had always been entirely informal and that the only record taken, or supposed to be taken, was the letter in which the Prime Minister informed the King of the course of the discussion and of its general conclusion.[1] It appears, however, from records discovered by Sir John Fortescue in the Windsor Library, that minutes were, in fact, regularly kept in George III's and George IV's time, while Lord Hankey, from whose *Diplomacy by Conference* I have borrowed freely in this lecture, quotes one instance as late as 1839. This had long ago been forgotten when the late Lord Salisbury could speak of the absence of all record as 'a fundamental requirement of the Cabinet system' which 'could only be made completely effective if the flow

[1] As regards individual differences of opinion, Disraeli frequently reported these to the Queen. Gladstone regarded it as 'base and treacherous' to disclose them. In modern practice I understand Prime Ministers have on occasion reported the views of individual members on questions of importance.

of suggestions which accompanied it attained the freedom and fulness which belonged to private conversations—members must feel themselves untrammelled
by any consideration of consistency with the past or
self-justification in the future'.[1] This defence of a comparatively recent tradition ignored the distinction between the undesirability of keeping a note of individual
expressions of opinion and the disadvantage of having
no record of the general conclusion arrived at and no
regular means of seeing that it is carried out. In the
absence of such a record there was always the danger
of members, through bias, inattention, deafness or
somnolence, going away with entirely different ideas
of what was decided and, where their own departments
were concerned, varying or even disregarding definite
conclusions which did not agree with their own views.

It was one of the troubles of the Cabinet of 1874–
80 that Lord Derby, as Foreign Secretary, habitually
watered down Cabinet decisions, and a special Cabinet
Committee had to be set up to keep him in order.
Typical of what must often have occurred is the following letter from Lord Hartington's private secretary to
Mr. Gladstone's private secretary in July 1882:[2]

'Harcourt and Chamberlain have both been here this
morning and *at* my chief about yesterday's Cabinet proceedings. They cannot agree about what occurred. There
must have been some decision, as Bright's resignation shows.
My Chief told me to ask you what the devil *was* decided for
he be damned if he knows. Will you ask Mr. G. in more
conventional and less pungent terms?'

[1] *Life of Lord Salisbury*, by Lady Gwendolen Cecil, ii. 223.
[2] Quoted from Lord Hankey's *Diplomacy by Conference*, which gives
many other instances confirming the frequency of serious misunderstandings in the absence of any record.

The split over Home Rule in Mr. Gladstone's Cabinet in 1885 was similarly accompanied by a series of misunderstandings. The whole tariff controversy in 1903 need never have arisen in so controversial a form if Mr. Ritchie in framing his budget had not, in Mr. Joseph Chamberlain's absence in South Africa, disregarded what the latter believed to have been a definite and practically unanimous Cabinet decision taken before he left, in favour of a preferential remission of the shilling corn registration duty. Here, again, subsequent correspondence throws a curious light on the danger of leaving important issues to unrecorded conversations. After the Balfour Cabinet had been largely broken up by resignations, Mr. Chamberlain wrote to the Duke of Devonshire on 21 September 1903:

'What did I ask you before I went to South Africa? That you should retain the shilling duty and give a drawback to Canada. I thought you had all, except Ritchie, accepted this policy. While I was slaving my life out, you threw it over as of no importance, and it is to this indifference to a great policy, which you yourself had accepted, that you owe the present position.'

The following sentences from the Duke of Devonshire's reply are characteristic, both of the situation and of the writer:

'As you know, I am rather deaf, and, I am afraid, sometimes inattentive. I certainly altogether failed to understand that . . . a decision was even provisionally taken of such importance as that to which you refer, and it must have been taken after very little discussion.'

The weaknesses of the system were summed up by Lord Curzon in the House of Lords (19 June 1918):

'There was no agenda, there was no order of business. Any Minister requiring to bring up a matter either of departmental or of public importance had to seek the permission of the Prime Minister to do so. No one else, broadly speaking, was warned in advance. It was difficult for any Minister to secure an interstice in the discussion in which he could place his own case. No record whatever was kept of our proceedings, except the private and personal letter written by the Prime Minister to the Sovereign, the contents of which, of course, are never seen by anybody else. The Cabinet often had the very haziest notion as to what its decisions were; and I appeal not only to my experience, but to the experience of every Cabinet Minister who sits in this House and to the records contained in the memoirs of half a dozen Prime Ministers in the past, that cases frequently arose when the matter was left so much in doubt that a Minister went away and acted upon what he thought was a decision which subsequently turned out to be no decision at all, or was repudiated by his colleagues. No one will deny that a system, however embedded in the traditions of the past and consecrated by constitutional custom, which was attended by these defects, was a system which was destined immediately it came into contact with the hard realities of war, to crumble into dust at once . . . and to make a long story short, I do not think anyone will deny that the old Cabinet system had irretrievably broken down, both as a war machine, and as a peace machine.'

The difficulties at all times inherent in these casual methods inevitably increased with the steady growth of the size of the Cabinet from ten or twelve to twice that number, and with the ever increasing volume and complexity of the work to be done. Above all, when it came to facing the need for serious preparation for war and to the actual conduct of war itself, the inadequacy of discussion by a score of civilians without any expert guidance became only too obvious. It was to meet the situation revealed by the South African War and to face the dangers now clearly looming ahead that Mr. Balfour in 1904 created the Committee of Imperial Defence, on the lines recommended by the Esher Committee. This was a purely consultative and advisory body consisting of the Prime Minister and such Ministers and experts as he might summon for the occasion, though normally including both ministerial and technical representatives of the Fighting Services. Its importance lay, firstly, in the fact that it was concerned with the future rather than with immediate day to day problems; secondly, in its bringing politicians and experts together for practical discussions; and last, but not least, that it had a secretarial staff, agenda, minutes, and records. Under a succession of able secretaries, and notably under Sir Maurice (now Lord) Hankey, the Committee of Imperial Defence, working largely through a network of sub-committees, secured for this country and, indeed, for the whole Empire, as effective a preparation for war, when it came in 1914, as was possible under a military system based, not on any strategical considerations, but on our peace garrisons and the exigencies of voluntary recruiting.

For over two years Mr. Asquith continued to try to direct the war on conventional Cabinet lines. The attempt to secure greater efficiency and promptitude of action by delegating the conduct of operations to a small War Council eventually broke down owing to divided counsels and the strain of frequent meetings on overworked departmental Ministers. In February 1916 the late Sir Mark Sykes and myself put forward in debate the revolutionary suggestion that the only

Government that could carry on the war was a Cabinet of four or five men entirely free from all departmental responsibilities and in a position to give their whole time to the thinking out, shaping and execution of policy. Mr. Asquith pooh-poohed the absurd proposal. But the idea caught on and was adopted wholeheartedly by Mr. Lloyd George when he formed his War Cabinet at the end of the year. At the same time, with equal disregard of tradition, he took over for the purposes of the Cabinet, lock, stock, and barrel, the whole of the methods and apparatus of the Committee of Imperial Defence. Sir Maurice Hankey became the first Secretary to the Cabinet, a post in which he rendered invaluable service in the war and played a vital, if deliberately inconspicuous, part in the establishment of Cabinet procedure over many years.

The War Cabinet of 1916 consisted of five members.[1] Only one of these, Mr. Bonar Law, then Chancellor of the Exchequer, held an administrative post, but his inclusion was due to the fact that he was leader of the Conservative party and deputy leader in the House of Commons. This freedom from routine enabled the Cabinet to meet every morning for five days of the week and oftener without disorganizing the work of departmental Ministers who only attended when their own particular business was affected. It afforded much more

[1] Mr. Lloyd George, Lord Milner, Lord Curzon, Mr. Bonar Law, and Mr. Henderson. Between the Imperial War Cabinet sessions of 1917 and 1918 General Smuts stayed behind and was made a full member of the War Cabinet while still a member of General Botha's Cabinet in South Africa and while not a member of either House in this country, an unusual example of the elasticity of our Constitution. Lord Balfour, as Foreign Secretary, while technically not a member, was, in fact, in continuous attendance.

time for the discussion and thinking out of policy among members of the War Cabinet, especially on those occasions when the War Cabinet, as such, met entirely by itself. Besides Ministers directly affected their expert advisers and, more particularly, the Chiefs of Staff habitually attended, another innovation taken directly from the working of the Committee of Imperial Defence. Members of the War Cabinet presided over all important ministerial committees, with the exception of a standing committee on Home Affairs presided over by the Home Secretary. Their higher authority and the time at their disposal enabled them to play a dominating part both in shaping the conclusions of such committees and in securing their acceptance by the Cabinet. The decisions were those of the Cabinet and not compromises between conflicting departmental views.

Every Cabinet meeting was attended by Sir Maurice Hankey and, except on a few occasions of extreme secrecy, by one or more of his assistant secretaries whose task it was immediately after the meeting to draft for him the minutes, which were then circulated early that same afternoon for concurrence or amendment by the Prime Minister and other Ministers concerned. However inconclusive the discussion Hankey insisted that the minute on each subject should, if at all possible, be made to end in a definite decision, a task calling at times for no little ingenuity and even inventiveness. It was only very occasionally, however, that Ministers queried the conclusions thus arrived at. The minutes at first included fairly full records of individual views. Subsequently the sounder practice prevailed of only summarizing the arguments used, exception being made of the case laid before the Cabinet by the Minister responsible for raising a subject, or by experts in attendance, and, very rarely, of a formal note of dissent. The next and in some ways the most important task of the secretaries was to follow up the conclusions and find out what action was being taken. This not only ensured the due fulfilment of Cabinet policy but also kept the Civil Service in closer contact with Cabinet policy 'on the official level'. A similar procedure was followed in the case of all Cabinet Committees. The Secretariat similarly provided the nucleus of the British Government's staff at the Imperial War Cabinet and at international conferences.

Apart from the purely routine secretarial work, Sir Mark Sykes and myself, as political assistant secretaries, were encouraged to contribute our quota of thinking ahead in the shape of memoranda circulated to the Cabinet, while Mr. Lloyd George subsequently created a small secretariat or thinking department of his own, known from its location in the garden of 10 Downing Street as the 'Garden Suburb', of which Philip Kerr (afterwards Lord Lothian) and W. G. S. Adams were the most active and influential members. These informal adjuncts to the work of the War Cabinet served a useful purpose even if they sometimes impinged on departmental preserves and shocked official proprieties. It was only Mr. Lloyd George's tendency to conduct foreign policy through the 'Garden Suburb' that at times created serious inconvenience.

For a few months after the war the attempt was made to maintain the War Cabinet system. But the force of tradition and the claims of individuals proved too strong, and by November 1919 Mr. Lloyd George reverted to a typical pre-war Cabinet of twenty. The secretarial machinery, however, remained, and has been steadily perfected since, an imperative necessity in view of the ever increasing flood of memoranda and telegrams circulated to the Cabinet, the ever growing volume of problems to be dealt with, and the steady development of the use made of Cabinet Committees. Meanwhile as early as July 1917 Mr. (now Lord) Addison, as Minister of Reconstruction, had appointed a strong committee under Lord Haldane to report on the whole 'Machinery of Government'. Their report, without entering into the question of the type of Cabinet to be adopted in future, urged that the Cabinet should be kept small, not exceeding twelve at most, and that the novel feature of the Secretariat should be retained.

The chief concern of the Haldane Report was, however, with the work of the departments. With regard to this their recommendations fell under two main heads. The first and, in their view, most important, was that in all departments there should be a more definite recognition of the duty of investigation and thought as preliminary to action. Admitting that in civil administration the elaboration of policy cannot be so readily distinguished from the business of administration as in the Fighting Services, they urged better provision for inquiry and research in all departments and the supervision of these functions by a special Department of Research.

The second recommendation was that the illogical and overlapping growth of departments should be limited by a reallocation of duties in accordance with the nature of the service rendered. From this point of view the Report divided the business of Government under ten main heads: Finance, National Defence,

External Affairs, Research and Information, Production, Employment, Supplies, Education, Health, and Justice.[1] The Report did not, as is sometimes suggested, advocate that each of these divisions should be under a single Minister. With three Service Ministers grouped under Defence, with Foreign Affairs, Dominions, India, and Colonies under External Affairs, and with Agriculture, Transport, and Commerce under Production, at least seventeen or eighteen departments must have been envisaged.

Some of the reallocation recommended was subsequently put into practice, and is reflected in the existing Ministries of Transport, Health, Labour, and Supply. To a very limited extent, too, the provision of information and research sections has been introduced in some departments, but nowhere in the sense of creating anything like a General Staff section for the study of future needs and eventualities. For the rest, there is still much necessary work to be done in carrying out the spirit, if not the actual letter, of the Haldane recommendations.

So far as preparation for war is concerned the vitally important Ministry of Supply or Munitions was dropped, only to be revived in 1939 on the very eve of war. The only really fruitful step taken between the two wars was the strengthening of the Committee of Imperial Defence by the creation in 1923 of the Chiefs of Staff Committee. In the absence, however, of a chairman, not only empowered to do what the Chiefs of Staff themselves could not do, namely, insist on effective co-ordination on issues where the Services differed, but recognized as, in effect,

[1] From the point of view of the actual work of the Civil Service a correct allocation of duties between departments means a substantial saving of time spent on inter-departmental committees.

the ministerial chief of the three General Staffs, the arrangement failed to achieve all that it might have done. The appointment in 1936 of a Minister to co-ordinate defence at large with no department of his own served little purpose. Full value was only secured from the Chiefs of Staff Committee when Mr. Churchill became his own Minister of Defence and the Chiefs of Staff became in effect his direct subordinates. In this way the Chiefs of Staff Committee, assisted by Joint Intelligence and Planning Staffs set up in the Cabinet Offices, provided a much better instrument for dealing with strategical problems than Mr. Lloyd George had at his disposal in the First World War. That this instru-ment was in the hands of one with a far greater ex-perience of military affairs and a far surer and happier touch in dealing with service men is a point I need not elaborate.

The experience gained in the last war has now been embodied in the creation of a Minister of Defence who is, under the Prime Minister, as official chairman of the Defence Committee,[1] and subject to final Cabinet authority, responsible for defence policy and the only permanent representative of defence policy in the Cabinet. The new Minister of Defence will be chair-man of a Standing Committee of the three Service Ministers and of inter-Service Committees on Personnel

[1] The dropping of the designation Imperial Defence is, apparently, not intended to involve any change of function, but only to be a con-cession to the nervous shrinking from the adjective 'Imperial' which has characterized the attitude of certain Governments of the Empire in recent years. The objection might have been more intelligible if the committee had been called Imperial Committee and had suggested a body under collective control. But as attached to the word 'Defence' the adjective only stated the obvious fact that the defence of the United Kingdom cannot be considered in isolation from that of the Empire.

and Supply attached to it. But the really important aspect of the change is that he will not be a mere co-ordinator, but will be directly in charge of a small Ministry of his own which will from the outset include the Combined Operations Headquarters, the Joint Intelligence Bureau, the Imperial Defence College, and the Committee of Defence Research. He is entitled to preside over the meetings of the Chiefs of Staff Committee and, indeed, the range of his functions should make him, what Mr. Churchill was, the real ministerial chief of the Chiefs of Staff, so far at least as strategic policy concerned.

Definitely superior as was the strategical equipment of government in the late war, I would not be prepared to say the same of the Cabinet organization as a whole. There was no War Cabinet in the sense of a small body free from administrative routine tasks and able to concentrate whole-heartedly on policy and on supervision. The designation was applied to eight of the more important Ministers who attended all Cabinet meetings throughout and in whose name all decisions were taken. Though Mr. Churchill's War Cabinet met somewhat less frequently than Mr. Lloyd George's, the strain on those who were also heads of great departments was very heavy.[1] Those who were without departments were, however, free to preside over committees, and a standing committee under the Lord President performed a very useful function. The whole set-up was, in fact, a compromise between the 1916 system and an ordinary peace-time Cabinet. It suited Mr. Churchill,

---

[1] The Churchill War Cabinet met 919 times in just over five years. The Lloyd George Cabinet met 490 times in 1917 and 1918, including Imperial War Cabinet meetings.

and in these matters a Prime Minister's idiosyncrasies and the personal material available count for more, perhaps, than the formal organization. Including the nucleus of eight, the total number of Ministers of 'Cabinet rank' grew by the middle of 1945 to forty-one. The present Government have reverted to a 'normal' peace-time Cabinet of eighteen with another fourteen Ministers of Cabinet rank outside.

The question we may now fairly ask ourselves is whether this 'normal' Cabinet machinery is capable of meeting the ever growing demands of administration and policy in a period of dangerous international stresses and of far-reaching political, social, and economic reconstruction at home and in the Empire? For my own part I would unhesitatingly affirm that it is not, and that until it is made capable of meeting the demands upon it there will be no effective leadership either in Parliament or in action outside, and a growing danger of a loss of confidence in our whole system of government. It is my profound conviction, based on a good many years of practical experience, that a Cabinet consisting of a score of overworked departmental Ministers is quite incapable of either thinking out a definite policy, or of securing its effective and consistent execution. I cannot do better than repeat to-day what I wrote more than ten years ago about the way in which the normal Cabinet system works:

'We attempt to direct the affairs of a great nation by weekly meetings between departmental chiefs, all absorbed in the routine of their departments, all concerned to secure Cabinet sanction for this or that departmental proposal, all giving a purely temporary and more or less perfunctory attention to the issues brought up by other departments.

Every Cabinet meeting is a scramble to get through the agenda in which the competition of departments for a place is varied by the incursion of urgent telegrams from abroad or of sudden questions in the House of Commons for which some sort of policy or answer must be improvised. The one thing that is hardly ever discussed is general policy. Nothing, indeed, is more calculated to make a Cabinet Minister unpopular with his colleagues, to cause him to be regarded by them as "Public Enemy No. 1", than a tiresome insistence on discussing general issues of policy, often controversial, when there are so many urgent matters of detail always waiting to be decided. The result is that there is very little Cabinet policy, as such, on any subject. No one has time to think it out, to discuss it, to co-ordinate its various elements, or to see to its prompt and consistent enforcement. There are only departmental policies. The "normal" Cabinet is really little more than a standing conference of departmental chiefs where departmental policies come up, from time to time, to be submitted to a cursory criticism as a result of which they may be accepted, blocked, or in some measure adjusted to the competing policies of other departments. But to a very large extent each department goes its own way, following its own bent and its own tradition, fighting the "Whitehall War" to the best of its ability. . . .

'The whole system is one of mutual friction and delay with, at best, some partial measure of mutual adjustment between unrelated policies. It is quite incompatible with any coherent planning of policy as a whole, or with the effective execution of such a policy. It breaks down hopelessly in a serious crisis where clear thinking over difficult and complex situations, definite decisions (not formulae of agreement) and swift and resolute action are required.'[1]

The same conclusion was summed up by the late

[1] *The Forward View*, pp. 443-5.

Professor Ramsay Muir in the following passage of his *How Britain is Governed*:

'The Cabinet has arrogated to itself, half blindly, a series of colossal responsibilities which it cannot meet, which it will not allow Parliament to tackle, and which are not met at all except in so far as they are assumed by the bureaucracy behind the cloak of Cabinet omnipotence.'

In a recent Romanes Lecture Sir John Anderson has suggested, as a solution to the problem, the more systematic development of the existing practice of Cabinet Committees. This would undoubtedly be of some help. But it will not carry us very far unless the structure and character of the Cabinet itself is altered, and unless regard is paid to the fundamental weakness of any system which does not make special provision for the framing of policy as such separated from routine day-to-day administration. It is a commonplace of scientific organization, long since recognized in the Fighting Services, that where the same persons are responsible for day-to-day administration as well as for the planning of policy to meet the remoter needs and uncertain eventualities of the future, the latter duty is bound to be neglected. Routine business is always more urgent and calls for less intellectual effort than sitting down to think seriously about something that may happen 'next year, sometime, never'. It is only by the creation of a separate policy department, a general staff, freed from administration as a whole, that it is possible to secure forethought and effective planning. The distinction between administration and policy may not, as the Haldane Committee pointed out, be quite so marked in civil as in military affairs,[1] where policy is concerned

[1] The organization required naturally varies with the character of

with so definite and at the same time uncertain an eventuality as war. But it is there all the same, and there can be no real efficiency in modern government unless it is clearly recognized and provision made to give effect to its requirements.

There is nothing very new in the point I am making. A shrewd observer of our Government from inside, Sir Henry Taylor, in his day a leading light of the Colonial Office and a poet and writer of some distinction, stated it far better than I can in a remarkable little book, *The Statesman*, published in 1836. What was true then is so much truer and more urgent to-day that I cannot forbear quoting him at some length:

'It is one business to do what must be done, another to devise what ought to be done. It is in the spirit of the British Government, as hitherto existing, to transact only the former business; and the reform which it requires is to enlarge that spirit so as to include the latter. . . .

'The current compulsory business he [i.e. a Minister] gets through as he may; some is undone, some is ill done; but at least to get it done is an object which he proposes to himself. But as to the inventive and suggestive portions of a Statesman's functions, he would think himself an Utopian dreamer if he undertook them: and such he would be if he undertook

each department. In the Fighting Services the work is divided between the various members of a Board or Council, and the Chiefs of Staff have no administrative functions outside planning, training, and operational movements and dispositions. Departments like the Foreign Office or India Office are essentially policy departments in which administration plays a secondary part, and in their case the Permanent Under Secretary is in effect the Chief of Staff as well as head of the administrative side. The separation between planning and current administration in such a department would naturally take place at a lower official level. In many of the domestic departments not the least important part of the information side of planning would be inquiry into the actual working of existing legislation and administration.

them in any other way than through a reconstitution and reform of his establishment. . . .

'This then is the great evil and want—that there is not within the pale of our government any adequately numerous body of efficient statesmen, some to be more externally active and answer the demands of the day, others to be somewhat more retired and meditative in order that they may take thought for the morrow. How great the evil of this want is, it may require peculiar opportunities of observation fully to understand and feel: but one who with competent knowledge should consider well the number and magnitude of those measures which are postponed for years or totally pretermitted, not for want of practicability, but for want of time and thought, could not choose, I think, but say within himself, that there must be something fatally amiss in the very idea of statesmanship on which our system of administration is based; or that there must be some mortal apathy at what should be the very centre and seat of life in a country.'

How is this great 'evil and want' to be cured without running into the opposite danger of a complete divorce between policy and administration? I can only put forward, for what they are worth, my own tentative suggestions, based on combining the recommendations of the Haldane Committee with the features found most useful in the Cabinet organization of the last thirty years.

At the apex of the whole structure, and as the necessary link between policy and administration, I would have a Cabinet of about half a dozen, all entirely free from ordinary departmental duties. This Cabinet would deal with current administrative questions, as did the War Cabinets of the last two wars, by bringing into its discussions the departmental Ministers directly affected.

But it should also have regular meetings definitely set aside for the discussion of future policy. The work of the former type of meetings would be expedited by standing and *ad hoc* committees, such as those outlined by Sir John Anderson, over which members of the Cabinet would preside with the advantage both of their higher authority and of their freedom from other routine work. For these no special staff would be required beyond the purely secretarial assistance provided by the Cabinet Secretariat.

But apart from co-ordinating and adjusting the current work of departments there should be, corresponding to the Defence Committee, a group of standing committees for the study of policy in the main fields of External Affairs, Economics, and Social Welfare, each with its own adequate research and planning staff. These staffs should not be self-contained bodies, but, like the Joint Intelligence and Planning Staffs developed in the last war, should be manned by members of the intelligence and planning staffs of their several offices at what is known in government circles as 'the official level'. As in the case of the Defence Committee, the Prime Minister should be the official chairman of each of these Policy Committees and preside over at least some of the more important meetings. At the same time, as has now been done in the case of Defence, he should appoint one of his colleagues as standing deputy chairman of each committee and acting head of its staff. The Cabinet Minister so appointed would be much more than a mere 'co-ordinator', in no position to overcome departmental obstruction and a mere fifth wheel to the coach, such as was the case with previous appointments for co-ordinating defence or for dealing with unemployment.

He would be the recognized Policy Minister for his group of departments, with the knowledge and authority derived from his regular handling of his subject-matter both on current affairs committees and on his Standing Policy Committee, and he would have his own staff behind him.[1]

Recent experience does not suggest that such a distinction between Ministers primarily responsible for the broad issues of policy and Ministers concerned primarily with administration need create any parliamentary difficulty. Mr. Churchill, as Minister of Defence in the domain of policy, dealt with the broad problems of strategy in respect of all the Services without detracting from the responsibility of the three Service Ministers or from the interest taken by Parliament in their work. It would, indeed, be all to the good if Parliament itself got into the habit of drawing a clearer distinction between policy and administration, and if great issues of policy and minor grievances of personnel, &c., were less jumbled together in the same debates. Nor does the experience of the working of the Joint Intelligence and Planning Staffs suggest that any insuperable strain was imposed on the departmental loyalty of their members as the result of their dual capacity. On the contrary, the more the staffs of the different offices are brought together in person on common tasks the less voluminous, protracted, and contentious, one might fairly expect, would be the normal routine of interdepartmental correspondence.

[1] On 10 March 1947 Sir Stafford Cripps announced the appointment of a joint planning staff to deal with the economic problems on very much the above lines, but without the ministerial co-ordination which seems to me essential.

On some, at any rate, of the great issues affecting our national security or less directly concerned with party politics, it would be in accordance both with the spirit of our Constitution and with precedent if the leaders of the Opposition of the day were more regularly associated with the discussions of these Standing Committees. This could be done, as has been the custom in inviting Dominion representatives to the Committee of Imperial Defence, at special meetings. Or it might be done, as Lord Hankey has recently suggested,[1] by the creation of special sub-committees at which Dominion and Opposition representatives would be regularly represented.

The scheme which I have suggested would not, I think, be open to the charge of creating a divorce between planning and administration. On the contrary the two would be kept in touch and integrated at all levels. The small Policy Cabinet would have continuously before it the views of the departmental Ministers, as they affected both administration and policy in their departments, not only at the Cabinet itself, but also through the proposed standing Policy Committees and through the various permanent and *ad hoc* committees dealing with current questions. Their planning staffs would not be isolated academic bodies, but integral parts of the departments with whose affairs they would be dealing. In the Fighting Services officers on the General Staff side all have to take their turn from time to time on ordinary executive or administrative duties, and a similar principle could apply in other departments where separate planning or research branches were set up. At the same time the importance of the planning and policy function would be recognized at

[1] *Diplomacy by Conference*, ch. ix.

every level. The Cabinet Ministers charged with co-ordinating duties would do so primarily from the policy point of view. This would meet what to my mind is the conclusive objection to the small Cabinet of super-Ministers, each directly responsible for the administration, as well as the policy, of a group of departments, which has often been advocated. For, in the absence of a clear distinction between the functions of policy and administration, these would tend to be even more overburdened, in Cabinet and in Parliament, with administrative responsibilities, and even less capable of thinking ahead than the members of the present type of Cabinet. Nor could such a system cope nearly so satisfactorily with the continuous creation of new departments necessitated by modern conditions in peace and even more in war.

It should be possible, on the lines which I have suggested, to secure a real co-ordination of the work of departments in the light of coherent policies thought out beforehand in place of the weak compromises, post-ponements, and fluctuations which have so often resulted from the attempt to reconcile conflicting departmental policies as and when a problem has obtruded itself upon the attention of an overworked Cabinet. One might give many instances. A typical one is Palestine, where the Foreign Office, anxious to avoid immediate trouble with the Arab States, has generally for many years now been at variance with such constructive policy as the Colonial Office has wished to carry out, with results with which we are only too painfully familiar to-day.

There is one department, indeed, which, more than any other, needs under present-day conditions to have

its policy co-ordinated—I might even say subordinated
—to the needs of Cabinet policy as a whole; I mean the
Treasury. In the *laissez-faire* era, when the supreme
object of Government was to do as little as possible and
to take as little as possible from the taxpayer of the
money that would otherwise 'fructify in his pocket', it
was only natural that the keeping down of expenditure
as such was regarded as the most important function
of administration. To-day, when expenditure on a vast
scale is not only unavoidable for such purposes as
defence, but regarded as desirable in itself for social
purposes, the supreme object must be the encouragement of the productive energies by which alone that
expenditure can be sustained. The tradition under
which the field of monetary policy and taxation, pro-
foundly affecting the whole economic life of the nation,
has been treated as a special Treasury preserve, with
which Cabinet colleagues have not been supposed to
meddle, is incompatible with that object. It is essential
to-day that the departments concerned with production, with industry and commerce, with agriculture
and mining, should have an effective and, indeed, a
dominant voice in laying down the broad principles
of monetary, tariff, and taxation policy of which the
technical working out and operation naturally fall to
the Treasury.

We cannot afford a repetition of the disastrous policy
of deflation pursued after 1919 in order to screw sterling
up to the old gold parity, or allow the immense possibilities of our export trade in motor vehicles to be
paralysed by Treasury insistence that no change in the
basis of motor taxation could be sanctioned which
involved an immediate reduction in the revenue from

that particular tax. The Treasury should be, not the master, but the faithful steward of the productive departments, carrying out the policies which most help them and then vigilantly seeing to it that all the purposes sanctioned by Parliament and the Cabinet are fulfilled with the utmost economy, i.e. that the nation should get the fullest value for every shilling spent.

The tradition that, in the pursuit of economy, it was the Treasury's rightful business to find reasons, good or bad, for whittling down in detail and delaying all demands for expenditure, even after they had been expressly sanctioned by the Cabinet or by Parliament, lingered long into the present century. It is only in recent times that a broader outlook has prevailed without, I believe, any detriment to true economy. The creation in recent years of a Methods Branch concerned with the true economy of proper administrative methods and equipment marks a useful advance in the right direction. On the other hand, the acceptance in the last generation of the view that the permanent head of the Treasury is the head of the whole Civil Service and the ultimate authority, under the Prime Minister, in all senior appointments has undoubtedly tended to create a certain subservience on the part of other departments towards the Treasury which is not calculated to make for initiative and independence. It would be the natural consequence of the changes which I have advocated for the general control of the Civil Service to be taken out of the hands of the Treasury and placed under the Prime Minister or one of his colleagues in the Policy Cabinet.

Whether our budgetary and estimates system in its present form is conducive to real economy is another question. I have never myself understood why a proper annual balance-sheet, distinguishing capital and current expenditure, and allowing for the carry forward of expenditure once sanctioned, could not be reconciled with parliamentary procedure, or why parliamentary procedure should not be altered to meet modern needs. Parliamentary control of finance has, indeed, as I have pointed out earlier, become largely a fiction, and a business-like statement of the real position might revive parliamentary interest in finance as such.

The setting up of a separate Ministry of Research advocated by the Haldane Report would, I think, be unnecessary under the scheme which I have suggested. It suffers, moreover, from a certain weakness underlying that Report in that it fails to recognize sufficiently that intelligence and research lose much of their value as a contribution to action unless they are closely linked with planning and policy. This, indeed, was the defect of the Economic Advisory Committee set up by Mr. Baldwin and further developed by Mr. MacDonald. My own experience of military organization has convinced me that the closest co-operation and integration of Intelligence and Operational staffs is essential both for securing the right intelligence and for sound planning. There is, of course, an important field of general research, occupied by such bodies as the Council of Scientific and Industrial Research, the Central Statistical Office, the new Central Office for Information, and the Medical and Agricultural Research Councils, not to speak of the future body which is to deal with Atomic Research, which naturally falls outside the scope of purely departmental research and planning. The general supervision of these bodies might very well be assigned to one of the members of the Policy Cabinet. But it is important that their work should be closely co-ordinated with the planning side of the departments concerned and that they should not attempt to carry out essentially departmental functions.

In dealing with the actual organization of the departments themselves the Haldane Report, in addition to its main emphasis on the importance of creating information and research sections in each department, laid great stress on the creation and development of Advisory Committees to secure contact with the public affected and to broaden the outlook of the Civil Service itself. To quote from the Report:

'The preservation of the full responsibility of Ministers for executive action will not, in our opinion, ensure that the course of administration which they adopt will secure and retain public confidence, unless it is recognized as an obligation upon Departments to avail themselves of the advice and assistance of advisory bodies so constituted as to make available the knowledge and experience of all sections of the community affected by the activities of the Department.' (§ 34.)

'So long as advisory bodies are not permitted to impair the full responsibility of Ministers to Parliament, we think that the more they are regarded as an integral part of the normal organization of a Department, the more will Ministers be enabled to command the confidence of Parliament and the public in their administration of the services which seem likely in an increasing degree to affect the lives of large sections of the community.' (§ 37.)

Since then there has been a great development in the use made by government departments of advisory bodies of all kinds, in the shape both of standing advisory committees of a general character, and still more of

committees set up to deal, either temporarily or permanently, with specific problems. This, over and above
the committees of inquiry, Joint Select Committees, or
Royal Commissions set up by the Government as such.[1]
My own impression is that full value will only be secured
from outside co-operation when the departments have
themselves organized each their own General Staff side
and have a clearer idea of what they are looking for and
where to find it.

That brings me to the question of the effect upon our
departmental organization and, indeed, on the Constitution itself of a very wide extension of the principle
of the nationalization of industries. In this connexion
the views of the Haldane Committee derive importance
not only from the political views of the chairman
but also from the fact that one of its members was
Mrs. Sidney Webb, to whose studies of the social and
constitutional problems raised by Socialist policy I
referred in my last lecture. The Report regards it as
a deduction from its main principle of the division
of departments according to services rendered that
nationalized industries should not be under departments which are concerned with rendering services to,
or regulating the operations of, citizens in their private
capacity.

'A combination in the same Ministry of the administration of any considerable State enterprise, involving the

---

[1] A very valuable detailed account of all the developments in this
field up to 1939, based on the work of an informal committee of leading Civil Servants, is given in *Advisory Bodies*, by R. V. Vernon and
N. Mansergh. A further development in connexion with industrial planning was foreshadowed by Sir S. Cripps on 10 March 1947 to take the
shape of a small board on which representatives of both sides of industry
will co-operate with the proposed Joint Planning Staff.

direct employment of labour on a large scale, the extensive purchase of supplies of many sorts, and possibly equally extensive sales to the public, with the duty of stimulating, regulating and controlling private enterprises in the same or cognate industries or services, is open to the gravest objection.' (§ 26.)

'A Department responsible for the direct employment of large numbers of men and women is not likely to be implicitly trusted either by employers or by employed if it is charged also with the function of determining the conditions of employment in private or municipal enterprise. . . . A Ministry itself engaged in production for the satisfaction of private consumers will hardly be trusted either by other manufacturers or by the public, if it is charged also with protecting the consumers from adulteration or excessive prices, or with determining the conditions under which competing products shall be permitted to be manufactured or imported.' (§ 27.)

This stipulation is, indeed, not merely one of practical convenience, but of constitutional importance. For it is of the essence of a constitution based on the Reign of Law that both legislation and administration should treat all citizens equally, and that government as such should be above all suspicion of partiality or prejudice in its actions. The difficulty is only partly met by delegating the detailed execution of a policy of nationalization to a council or board, and it is not easy to see, without further practical experience, what safeguards can best protect the rights of the subject to equal or, at least, equitable treatment. The more such councils or boards are given real freedom from departmental and ministerial control and the more their directorates approximate to those of ordinary business concerns and not to bureaucratic offices, the easier it will be, one might hope, for both Parliament and the public to insist on their operations conforming to that essential principle. From that point of view there might be much to be said, as an alternative method of securing the essential objects of nationalization, for the State acquiring whatever shareholding might be necessary in the industries selected, but retaining the ordinary structure, methods, incentives and obligations of private enterprise. Such co-ordination or amalgamation as might be required could then be carried out under holding boards appointed by the Minister concerned. In any case, whatever the organization selected it would be essential that Parliament should be kept fully informed by an annual report as well as by annual accounts, and should be afforded adequate opportunity for debate.

The immense change which has taken place, and is continuing to take place in the functions of government, must necessarily also affect not only the numbers[1] but the character and, therefore, the conditions of service of the higher Civil Service. The essential function of that service in the past has been regulative. That function can never be dispensed with. Our whole parliamentary system of debate and question necessitates the closest scrutiny of detailed methods, and the faithful recording of precedents and of the back history of every case. At the same time it will be more and more necessary to encourage the creative and constructive side of the work

---

[1] The total strength of the Civil Service rose from 296,648 in 1926 to 338,604 in 1936 and 376,491 in 1938. It stood at 695,950 in April 1946, and does not seem likely to fall below 500,000 in future. The total figure for employees of the National Government was given by Sir S. Cripps on 10 March 1947 as 1,016,000 (including 615,000 Post Office and industrial employees), while local government employees amounted to 1,014,000

of departments. Nor can there be any harm in that so long as government on the ministerial side retains effective initiative and control, and so long as Parliament is free to give adequate attention to what is happening.

It would, indeed, be a mistake to imagine that there is not already much initiative and creative thought in the departments, or that government policy in the past has not owed much to men like the late Sir Robert Morant or Lord Beveridge. The work of the great departments of State is, indeed, normally a close co-operation between the technical knowledge of the Civil Service and the ideas engendered in it by long and intimate experience of the subject-matter from within and the broader political outlook of Ministers. Sir William Harcourt put it cynically when he said that 'the value of political heads of departments is to tell the officials what the public will not stand'. He might have added that it also lies in the political Minister's greater ability to expound and defend the views and needs of his department in ways which will carry most weight with his colleagues. Lord Kitchener's incapacity to do this was a striking justification of the value of a civilian War Minister.

Such a development would naturally be strengthened by a reorganization of Cabinet and departmental work which gave real scope to research and planning. At the same time the question will have to be faced whether the present conditions of service, appealing naturally to men of high ability, but also to those inclined to think of life in terms of security of tenure, and leading to the highest positions only at a time when, in most men, the creative and driving spirit has weakened, are necessarily best suited to secure the type required. A much shorter minimum time-qualification for pension or, in many branches, an accruing capital payment in lieu of pension, might well prove more attractive to ambitious recruits, by ensuring more opportunities for able men to take up congenial work outside, while at the same time facilitating earlier retirement for those who are no longer up to the highest standard required. It would in both respects make for speedier promotion and earlier responsibility in the Service itself.

I have not attempted to discuss the working of that wide and immensely important field of the machinery of government which comes directly under the local authorities. The essential principle of that machinery is to be sought in the interaction between democratic local interest and local public spirit on the one side with stimulation, guidance, and inspection from the central departments through the system of financial subvention first introduced by Sir Robert Peel in order to raise the standard of efficiency of the local police forces. This method of subvention was considerably modified when, now some eighteen years ago, the system of proportionate grants in aid was converted into one of block grants taking more account of the needs of different localities than of their rateable capacity. Nor have I attempted to touch upon the equity or suitability of our rating system on which local finance is so largely based, or upon the question of the ideal areas for the carrying out of some of the functions, e.g. those in connexion with the administration of our National Health policy, for which existing local government areas are not suitable. I need only emphasize the part that local government plays in maintaining that continuous interest in public affairs which is the mainspring of our Constitution.

In conclusion, looking ahead, I can only repeat my

profound conviction that we cannot afford to carry on with the hand-to-mouth methods of the past, but must somehow finds ways and means by which to bring into our machinery of government that element of planning and forethought by which alone our statesmen can give leadership in Parliament and to the nation in dealing with the immense tasks of social and economic recon-struction before us and, even more, in facing dangers confronting our very existence. There are certain lines in George Meredith's *England before the Storm* which are even more true to-day than when written nearly ninety years ago:

> Would she to sainted forethought vow
> A space before the thunders flood,
> That martyr of its hour might now
> Spare her the tears of blood.

IV

THE EVOLUTION OF THE BRITISH COMMONWEALTH[1]

IN my first lecture I analysed the process of evolution by which our present-day British Constitution has come into being through the interaction and progressive integration of two historically and constitutionally distinct elements, the Crown and the Nation. In that process Parliament has been the meeting-point and focus in which, after centuries of alternating struggles for supremacy, the two were ultimately fused in the system which we know as responsible government. In this last lecture I propose to trace the not dissimilar evolution, by the gradual harmonization of conflicting forces and theories, of the constitution of that latest offspring of our political genius, the British Commonwealth of Nations.

In this case the original issue between Crown and Nation was first complicated and then entirely superseded by a further issue between two fundamentally different conceptions of the relation between this country and the British Empire overseas. The first was the legal conception of the executive and legislative omnipotence of the Crown in the Parliament of Britain over all British territories and over all His Majesty's subjects wherever residing. The second was the instinctive and irrepressible assertion by communities of British race and tradition of the right to be

[1] For more detailed information on the subject-matter of this chapter readers should consult *The British Commonwealth of Nations* by Duncan Hall for the period down to 1920, and *Speeches and Documents on the British Dominions* by Berriedale Keith for the period 1918–31.

governed and legislated for only subject to their own free consent—the assertion, in other words, of a claim to equality of political rights with the communities which had remained at home. The problem throughout has been how to reconcile that second conception with the maintenance of Imperial unity, a unity which, at one time, it was difficult to conceive as based on any other principle than that of a central authority omnipotent for, at any rate, the essential purposes of foreign policy and defence.

In the third quarter of the eighteenth century we, at Westminster, were still groping our way, more than half-unconsciously, towards the solution, by the device of responsible government, of the long controversy between Crown and Parliament. In the American Colonies that controversy was accentuated by a variety of factors. The Crown, as embodied in the Governor and his officials and surroundings, represented a distant, at times unsympathetic, more often uncomprehending authority, alien to the democratic social outlook of the colonists as well as to the republican tradition of New England Puritanism. What is more, the colonists had increasingly become conscious of the fact that they were not merely outlying British communities but a nation. Their development in the course of little more than a century had been amazing. There had been 'nothing in the history of mankind', as Burke truly said, to equal it. Their population relative to that of Great Britain was as large as that of the whole white population of all the Dominions to-day. They were sufficiently conscious of the part played by the old Imperial economic policy in promoting that prosperity, not to quarrel with the regulation by Parliament of their external trade.[1] But national as well as colonial pride was not prepared to brook the British Parliament's invasion of the field of direct taxation, even if it resulted from the colonists' own failure to find a constitutional method by which they could have fulfilled that national obligation to contribute to their own defence which British statesmen had vainly tried to secure from them.

It may well be that if the British Government had patiently persevered with that effort to bring about the union of the Colonies which it initiated at the Albany Conference of 1745, in spite of its rejection by all the Colonial Assemblies, and still more if it had also been capable of realizing the trend of its own constitutional evolution, secession might have been avoided. Unfortunately history is not shaped by retrospective foresight. The short-sighted logic of the extremists on both sides won the day and wrecked the hopes of an earlier British Commonwealth coming into being. It remained for Burke to preach for later generations the gospel of an Empire based on the loyalty begotten of freedom, and for the defeated and exiled remnant of loyalists in the Colonies to carry into the forest wilderness of Ontario

[1] The Declaration of Rights drawn up at Philadelphia just before the outbreak of the Revolution declared: 'From the necessity of the case and in regard to the mutual interest of both countries we cheerfully consent to the operation of such Acts of the British Parliament as are *bona fide* restrained to the regulation of our external commerce for the purpose of securing the commercial advantages of the whole Empire to the Mother Country and to its respective members.' Both Chatham and Burke, ardently as they vindicated the American cause, had no doubt that 'the inherent supremacy of the state in regulating and protecting the navigation and commerce of all her subjects, is necessary for the mutual benefit and preservation of every part' (Chatham, 20 Nov. 1777). On both sides of the Atlantic the regulation of trade was, in fact, regarded as essentially a policy of co-operation even if enforced by the predominant partner.

and Nova Scotia the unquenched torch of their faith that some time and somehow it would be possible to reconcile Empire unity with Colonial freedom. As for our subsequent relations with the American people, even if the constitutional link was snapped apart, there remained enough underlying unity, not only of language and culture, but of outlook on the problems of human liberty and of political and legal methods, to create a unique international relationship in which mutual criticism and mutual suspicion have, in every great emergency, been swept aside by a more deep-seated sense of a common interest.

It was a simpler and easier task that confronted British statesmanship when rebellion broke out in Canada in 1837. It is no detraction from Durham's greatness to point out that the responsible government which he recommended for the revolted colonies was by then something, not only fully understood, but already being regarded as self-evident at home. Moreover, in dealing with Canada, and subsequently with other colonies of British settlement, the British Government was confronted, not as in 1775, with a sensitive and, indeed, aggressive nationalism, but only with the more limited desire of small settler communities to conduct without interference the affairs that concerned them most. It was, indeed, a very limited and circumscribed field within which Durham himself contemplated the grant of self-government. Not only foreign policy and defence, but trade and the disposal of public lands, were to remain reserved to the Imperial authority at Westminster. Happily no statutory definition was ever given to that intention to set up what we should now call a system of diarchy. If it had been, the rift between

Colonial democracy and the autocratic power of a distant Crown and Parliament, temporarily closed by the grant of limited self-government, would inevitably have been reopened as soon as the Colonies felt the need for wider powers. Sooner or later, though peacefully, perhaps, rather than by violence, the Colonies would have gone the way of the United States.

As it was, each Colonial demand for wider powers, beginning with Canada's insistence on framing her own tariff, was conceded as it became urgent. At no point in the development from Colonial self-government to Dominion nationhood was there any direct conflict between local patriotism and loyalty to the Imperial connexion, no issue between Crown and People. On the contrary, the two instincts continually interacted and reinforced each other. The Confederation of Canada was a step equally inspired by Canadian and Imperial ideals, and the same may be said both of Australian Federation and of South African Union. The South African War and two World Wars each afforded a striking demonstration of the strength of the sentiment of Imperial unity, while each enhanced in every Dominion the sense of its own national distinctiveness and the determination to assert the recognition of its claim to independent nationhood. The same century that saw Europe broken up, and in the end shattered, by the struggle of emerging and conflicting nationalities saw the coming into being, across the oceans, of nations already to-day the equals of individual European Powers, not only without violent secession from the parent country, but building up in conjunction with it a new type of constitutional unity unknown to history.

Few, indeed, had any glimpse of these possibilities in

the England of a hundred years ago. For the doctrinaire believers in a British economic world-empire, Colonial responsibilities were burdens to be got rid of as expeditiously as possible, and Colonial self-government combined with free trade seemed the obvious method of doing so without fuss or friction. 'The Colonial system', wrote Cobden in 1842, 'can never be got rid of except by the indirect process of Free Trade which will gradually and imperceptibly loose the bonds which unite our Colonies to us by a mistaken notion of self-interest.' Nor, for a time, could Imperialists of the older authoritarian school see any other solution, much as they regretted it. It was in the Colonies that faith in Imperial unity remained undiscouraged, and it was from overseas, and more particularly from Canada, with its United Empire Loyalist tradition, that the reaction first spread to the Old Country.

Canadian Confederation may be regarded as the great turning-point in opinion here as well as overseas, as it was also the first positive step in the constitutional process which has led up to the Commonwealth as it stands to-day. Sir John Macdonald, indeed, did more, for he struck the keynote for all subsequent development in the double emphasis which he laid both upon Canadian nationality and upon the Crown as the symbol of Imperial unity. His purpose was 'the noble object of forwarding a great British Monarchy in connection with the British Empire and under the British Queen', and it was only Colonial Office fear of offending the United States that compelled him to abandon his plan for giving the new confederation the title of 'The Kingdom of Canada', and to substitute the word Dominion. He may rightly be regarded as the father of the great line of overseas statesmen, from his own junior contemporaries like Parkes in Australia and Rhodes in South Africa down to Laurier and Borden, Deakin and Seddon, Botha and Smuts, whose ideas have dominated the evolution of the Commonwealth.

Here in England the new belief in Empire which influenced British policy in the last quarter of the century was compounded of many strands of thought. There was the pride, voiced by writers like Seeley and Froude, in the virile life of the young British communities overseas. There was an equal pride, voiced by Kipling or by Milner's *England in Egypt*, in the task of direct administration and organization so successfully carried out by Englishmen in India and elsewhere. There was the sense of growing world competition, foreshadowed by the scramble for the partition of Africa. The Imperialist movement of the later decades of the last century has often been decried as a mere policy of aggressive self-assertion and economic exploitation. Its economic polities may have tended to reflect the middle-class capitalist outlook of the age. But it was on the whole a fine, generous movement based on a spirit of responsible trusteeship, which aimed both at protecting the growth of the young British nations and at raising the condition of backward races. In so far as it can be said to have had any very definite conception of the future constitutional relations with the self-governing Empire, it was in the direction of some kind of Imperial Federation which would recognize the Colonial demand for equality through participation in a central authority responsible for at least foreign policy and defence.

For Colonial public opinion, on the other hand, the

idea of Imperial Federation offered little attraction. In view of the immense disparity of population it would merely have meant heavy obligations with no real control over policy. Besides, the equality which overseas statesmen were already more or less consciously envisaging was not the equality of individual Canadians or Australians with individual Englishmen, but the equality of the younger nations, as nations, with the Mother Country. Their conception was not federation, with its rigid division of powers, but co-operation. And in thinking of co-operation they were less concerned with foreign policy and defence—for most of them still comparatively remote and unpredictable issues—than with mutual economic support in building up each other's welfare and the strength upon which defence and consequently foreign policy would in the long run depend.

They had deeply resented the abandonment of the moderate preferential system under which the Colonies had made such remarkable progress before 1846, not only because of the grave check to that progress, but even more because its leading exponents deliberately aimed at breaking up the Empire. It is impossible to understand the evolution of Empire relations over all this period unless we keep in mind that for Dominion statesmen Imperial Preference was, first and foremost, a constitutional issue, the obvious and primary method of asserting Imperial unity, while in this country, on the other hand, Free Trade was still a self-evident doctrine of almost religious sanctity, any 'deviation' from which, however slight and for however great an object, by anyone in a public position, meant instant excommunication.

It was in this atmosphere of a general desire to do something to promote Imperial unity, but with no agreement as to method, that advantage was taken of the presence of oversea representatives at Queen Victoria's Jubilee in 1887 to convene the first Colonial Conference. Federation was formally excluded from the agenda by the British Government which, on the other hand, also made it quite clear that it was not prepared to consider the Colonial demand for Imperial Preference. The British case for Colonial co-operation in defence made little appeal, partly no doubt because it was only conceived in terms of a monetary contribution to the British Navy, though the Australian colonies were induced to contribute £126,000 a year. But if the concrete results were slight there was still a feeling that something had been initiated which contained in itself the germ of a greater future, and Lord Salisbury's suggestion that the conference might prove 'the parent of a long progeniture' awakened sympathetic echoes. Once again the initiative was with Canada, and a second conference took place in Ottawa in 1894. This concentrated on the economic aspects of co-operation. Imperial Preference was endorsed by a formal resolution, from which only the United Kingdom and New South Wales dissented, while progress was made with the project of a jointly financed and owned Pacific Cable, finally settled in 1902.

The next two conferences were again the concomitants of two events in the life of the Monarchy which naturally brought the members of the British family together, the Diamond Jubilee of 1897 and King Edward VII's coronation in 1902. This time the main inspiration came from the vision and constructive statesmanship of Joseph Chamberlain. On the purely constitutional side his limitation of the invitation to Prime Ministers and, above all, his personal attitude towards them, marked a great step forward in the conception of co-operation between governments growing towards equality of status if still far from equality of stature. On the other hand, there was no response to his suggestion for the creation of an Imperial Council, though a resolution was passed in 1902 in favour of holding a conference every four years. Nor was much progress made on the side of defence. Canada refused to join the other Colonies in a small naval contribution, and only New Zealand endorsed the idea of a special body of troops earmarked by each Colony for Imperial service. Proud of their share in the South African War, the Colonies were still determined to reserve in their own hands their future course of action, though agreed on the training and organization of their forces on common lines with a view to co-operation if and when the need arose.

On the economic side Chamberlain tried to hold out the suggestion of an Imperial Zollverein or customs union with internal free trade, influenced, no doubt, by the hope that this might be more acceptable to British opinion and also, perhaps, by a more centralist conception of Empire unity. But the Colonial statesmen were not to be moved from their insistence, based essentially on constitutional grounds, on Imperial Preference. In the end Chamberlain was convinced that they were right, that the future of Empire unity must be based on co-operation, and not on any form of constitutional unification, and that the one line of approach to unity on which real progress could be made, and pave the way towards more effective co-operation on other lines, was that of Imperial Preference. Already in 1897 he had assented to Sir Wilfrid Laurier's request that the British Government should denounce the German and Belgian commercial treaties which, in the name of the Most Favoured Nation Clause, actually forbade Canada from granting an avowed unilateral preference to the United Kingdom. After the 1902 Conference he persuaded the Cabinet to agree to the remission on Empire wheat of the shilling registration duty on grain imposed during the South African War. Such a remission, insignificant in itself, might, he hoped, be taken as evidence of a genuine desire to meet the Colonial point of view without raising serious controversy at home, and set a precedent which might be cautiously developed.

Unfortunately, as I mentioned in my last lecture, this decision was forgotten or ignored in the absence of any Cabinet record, and Chamberlain on his return from South Africa on the eve of the budget found the Cabinet committed to dropping the whole duty. His subsequent eloquent appeal to the public to consider the possibility of some slight deviation from the rigid Free Trade dogma for the sake of Imperial unity precipitated years of political controversy in which the essentially constitutional aspect of Empire Preference was largely smothered by the more strictly economic issue between Free Imports and Protection.

In spite of its failure at home Chamberlain's campaign greatly encouraged the Colonial Governments, not only to follow Canada's lead in granting unreciprocated preferences to the Mother Country, but also to put forward their own suggestions for constitutional co-operation and to respond more readily to suggestions for co-operation in defence. So far, indeed, as preference was concerned all the eloquence of Deakin and Laurier at the Conference of 1907 could not open a door which, to use Mr. Churchill's phrase, the British Government had 'banged, bolted and barred' against any fiscal deviation. But the economic aspect of co-operation was kept alive by a variety of steps to improve communications, including a useful Merchant Shipping Conference in 1907, and by the appointment at the 1911 Conference of a Dominions Royal Commission—itself a constitutionally interesting precedent—to inquire into the possibilities of economic development in the Dominions. On the defence side real progress was marked by the holding, in 1909, of a special conference on Imperial Defence at which the Admiralty reluctantly accepted the principle of Dominion navies, by Dominion participation at meetings of the Committee of Imperial Defence and by the creation in each of the Dominions, at Sir Maurice Hankey's instigation, of Defence Committees and by the preparation of war books. No less important was the full discussion, at the Conference of 1911, not only of defence in all its aspects, but of the whole menacing field of foreign affairs, which was opened up by a notable speech of grave warning from Sir Edward Grey.

If the Dominions were united in their outlook on economics and defence, they differed when it came to the question of giving a more definite constitutional form to the by then accepted principle of co-operation. The keener Imperialists, led by Deakin, were eager to take relations with the Dominions out of the hands of the Colonial Office and entrust them to a joint secretariat. To this Mr. Asquith and Sir Wilfrid Laurier saw insuperable constitutional objections which do not seem to have occurred to anybody when the League of Nations Secretariat was established a few years later. But as a concession to the Dominion point of view the work in the Colonial Office was rearranged, and relations with the Dominions and arrangements for future conferences assigned to a separate branch. At the same time the term 'Dominion' was now formally substituted for Colonial Conference.

The whole principle of co-operation by conference was endorsed and embodied in definite shape by a resolution of the 1907 Conference recommending that the Imperial Conference should be held every four years with the Prime Minister of the United Kingdom as President and the Prime Ministers of the Dominions as *ex officio* members, together with the Secretary of State for the Colonies, who was to take the chair in the absence of the President.[1] Each government was to have one vote and normally not to have more than two representatives. The conference had

[1] The first part of the resolution runs as follows: 'That it will be to the advantage of the Empire if a Conference, to be called the Imperial Conference, is held every four years, at which questions of common interest may be discussed and considered as between His Majesty's Government and his Governments of the self-governing Dominions beyond the seas. The Prime Minister of the United Kingdom will be *ex officio* President, and the Prime Ministers of the self-governing Dominions *ex officio* members of the Conference. The Secretary of State for the Colonies will be an *ex officio* member of the Conference and will take the chair in the absence of the President. He will arrange for such Imperial Conferences after communication with the Prime Ministers of the respective Dominions. Such other Ministers as the respective Governments may appoint will also be members of the Conference—it being understood that, except by special permission of the Conference, each discussion will be conducted by not more than two representatives from each Government, and that each Government will have only one vote.'

now definitely ceased to be an appendage of the
Colonial Office and become, in Deakin's words, one
'between Governments and Governments, due recognition, of course, being had to the seniority and scope of
those Governments'. Provision was made at the same
time for the holding of subsidiary conferences as and
when found desirable.[1] As a further step to maintain
an authoritative link with the British Government
between conferences Sir Robert Borden, who succeeded
Sir Wilfrid Laurier in 1911, revived the practice,
initiated by Sir John Macdonald in the case of Sir
Charles Tupper in 1888, of making Sir George Perley
High Commissioner while still retaining his seat in the
Canadian Cabinet.

No attempt was made by Mr. Asquith to convene
the Imperial Conference for two years after the outbreak of the First World War. Mr. Lloyd George,
on taking office in December 1916, decided to make
good this omission. Here I hope I may be forgiven if I
introduce a note of personal reminiscence. I reached
London after being torpedoed at sea, completely un-
aware of the political situation, but just in time to hear
the new Prime Minister expounding to the House of
Commons the nature of the small War Cabinet which
he was setting up and for which I had contended nearly
a year before. When he went on to announce that he
proposed to convene a Special Imperial War Conference I said to myself, 'Why not an Imperial War
Cabinet?' Full of the idea I left the debate and went off
to urge it on Lord Milner, who immediately responded
and secured its acceptance at the War Cabinet's meeting

[1] e.g. besides those mentioned above the Education Conference,
1907, Copyright Conference, 1910, Surveyors Conference, 1911.

the next day. It was decided to hold this, not in substitution for, but in addition to the Imperial War
Conference, the distinction being that the Imperial
War Cabinet should consist only of Dominion Prime
Ministers sitting with the War Cabinet to deal with the
actual conduct of the war, while the conference should
consider inter-Imperial questions of a more general
character. The two bodies, in fact, sat on alternate
days, thus incidentally also affording time for the
British War Cabinet to attend to its own more specific
problems. For the first time India, in view of her
services in the war and in anticipation of her future
status, was invited to take part in both gatherings.[1]

The original idea was that only Dominion Prime
Ministers should attend the Imperial War Cabinet
meetings. As it happened, when the Dominion representatives arrived, it was found that the New Zealand
Coalition Government was in danger of breaking up if
Sir Joseph Ward was excluded from any meeting
attended by Mr. Massey, the Prime Minister. With
two representatives from New Zealand the major
Dominions obviously had to have at least two each, and
the Imperial War Cabinet lost something of the intimacy
originally aimed at. The difficulty was effectively
surmounted at subsequent Imperial War Cabinets and
Imperial Conferences by setting up a Prime Ministers' or
Heads of Delegations committee. The secretariat was,
in the first instance, provided by the War Cabinet
office. But Sir Maurice Hankey from the outset brought
the secretaries of the Dominion Ministers into the
organization, and at the further meetings of the

[1] Australia was unable to take part in this first Imperial War Cabinet,
but was represented by Mr. Hughes at subsequent sessions and in Paris.

Imperial War Cabinet and at all subsequent Imperial Conferences a joint secretariat was organized for the occasion.

The Imperial War Cabinet was an outstanding success. In so far as it worked as a single body of colleagues all concerned with the same end and each contributing the best of his individual judgement, it deserved the title of Cabinet as fully as any Cabinet that I have ever attended. It was bound together by a common sense of responsibility for a common cause even if it was not, in the narrower sense, collectively responsible to a single Parliament. It was, indeed, in the apt phrase used by Sir Robert Borden in the Canadian House of Commons, 'A Cabinet of Governments rather than of Ministers'. Nor could its constitutional significance have been better expressed than it was in an address given by Sir Robert Borden to the Empire Parliamentary Association while the Imperial War Cabinet was actually in session:

'It may be that in the shadow of the war we do not clearly realize the measure of recent constitutional development. . . . For the first time in the Empire's history there are sitting in London two Cabinets, both properly constituted and both exercising well defined powers. Over each of them the Prime Minister of the United Kingdom presides. One of them is designated as the "War Cabinet" which chiefly devotes itself to such questions touching the prosecution of the War as primarily concern the United Kingdom. The other is designated as the "Imperial War Cabinet", which has a wider purpose, jurisdiction and personnel. To its deliberations have been summoned representatives of all the Empire's self-governing Dominions. We meet there on terms of equality under the presidency of the First Minister of the United Kingdom; we meet there as equals, he is *primus inter pares*. Ministers from six nations sit around the council board, all of them responsible to their respective parliaments and to the people of the countries which they represent. Each nation has its voice upon questions of common concern and highest importance as the deliberations proceed; each preserves unimpaired its perfect autonomy, its self-government, and the responsibility of its own ministers to their own electorate. For many years the thought of statesmen and students in every part of the Empire has centred around the question of future constitutional relations; it may be that now, as in the past, the necessity imposed by great events has given the answer.'

After fourteen meetings of the Imperial War Cabinet between 20 March and 2 May 1917 the assembled Ministers unanimously agreed that the experiment had not only justified itself but should become a regular constitutional procedure. To quote Mr. Lloyd George's statement to the House of Commons on 17 May:

'The Imperial War Cabinet was unanimous that the new procedure had been of such service not only to all its members but to the Empire that it ought not to be allowed to fall into desuetude. Accordingly at the last session I proposed formally, on behalf of the British Government, that meetings of an Imperial Cabinet should be held annually or at any intermediate time when matters of urgent Imperial concern require to be settled, and that the Imperial Cabinet should consist of the Prime Minister of each of the Dominions, or some specially accredited alternate possessed of equal authority, and of a representative of the Indian people to be appointed by the Government of India. This proposal met with the cordial approval of the Overseas representatives, and we hope that the holding of an annual Imperial Cabinet to discuss foreign affairs and other aspects of Imperial policy will become an accepted convention of the British Constitution.

'I ought to add that the institution in its present form is extremely elastic. It grew, not by design, but out of the necessities of the war. The essence of it is that the responsible heads of the Governments of the Empire, with those Ministers who are specially entrusted with the conduct of Imperial policy, should meet together at regular intervals to confer about foreign policy and matters connected therewith, and come to decisions in regard to them which, subject to the control of their own Parliaments, they will then severally execute. By this means they will be able to obtain full information about all aspects of Imperial affairs, and to determine by consultation together the policy of the Empire in its most vital aspects, without infringing in any degree the autonomy which its parts at present enjoy.'

While this important practical development was in progress the Imperial War Conference debated at length the more fundamental problem of future constitutional relations, a debate summed up in the following resolution:

'The Imperial War Conference are of opinion that the readjustment of the constitutional relations of the component parts of the Empire is too important and intricate a subject to be dealt with during the War, and that it should form the subject of a special Imperial Conference to be summoned as soon as possible after the cessation of hostilities.

'They deem it their duty, however, to place on record their view that any such readjustment, while thoroughly preserving all existing powers of self-government and complete control of domestic affairs, should be based upon a full recognition of the Dominions as autonomous nations of an Imperial Commonwealth, and of India as an important portion of the same, should recognize the right of the Dominions and India to an adequate voice in foreign policy and in foreign relations, and should provide effective arrangements for continuous consultation in all important matters of common Imperial concern, and for such necessary concerted action founded on consultation, as the several Governments may determine.'

The Imperial War Cabinet and Imperial War Conference met again in June and July 1918. As the result of further constitutional discussions at the Conference the Imperial War Cabinet passed two important resolutions. The first emphasized the status of the Dominions by asserting the right of their Prime Ministers, 'as members of the Imperial War Cabinet', to communicate directly with the British Prime Minister on questions of Cabinet importance. The second declared their right to be represented 'at meetings of the Imperial War Cabinet to be held regularly between the plenary sessions' by a permanently resident or visiting Cabinet Minister. It was clear from the discussions, as well as from Mr. Lloyd George's speech already quoted, that the intention was to maintain the Imperial Cabinet as a permanent body in more or less continuous session.

In the interval between the sessions of the Imperial War Cabinet General Smuts remained in London as a member of the British War Cabinet while still also a member of General Botha's Cabinet in the South African Union. The fact deserves attention because of two interesting constitutional points involved. The first is that there is no inherent impossibility in a member of the Cabinet not being a member of either House of Parliament so long as no direct inconvenience arises. The second is the interchangeability of functions made possible by the existence of the common status of British subject. Sir Robert Borden, on occasion, represented the British Government on the Council of Ten and the Council of Four during the peace negotiations. Lord

Balfour in 1922 acted as South Africa's representative at the Washington Naval Conference, while Lord Cecil, on one occasion, represented the Union at Geneva.

The Imperial War Cabinet was reassembled after the Armistice in November and remained in continuous session, described when in Paris as the 'British Empire Delegation', until the signing of the treaty with Germany in June 1919. When it came to the peace negotiations the Dominions insisted on their right to individual representation as nations. This, for the first time, secured for them a recognized international status. What was far more important, however, in practice was that, in virtue of the British Empire Delegation, they were, in fact, part of the 'Big Four' who really decided. While the lesser so-called independent nations hung about outside the doors of the great, anxious as to what was being decided over their heads and eager to pick up any crumbs of information that might be vouchsafed to them, the Dominion representatives were not only able to keep in daily touch with the course of events, but to see to it that their point of view was effectively maintained on all issues that affected them. The Peace Treaties were signed by the Dominion representatives separately, as plenipotentiaries of the King as the 'High Contracting Party' for the whole Empire, and approved by resolution in each Parliament concerned before ratification. The Dominions and India joined the League of Nations as individual original members and individually undertook mandatory obligations to the League in respect of territories taken by them in the course of the war.[1]

[1] The list of original signatories to the Covenant placed the 'British Empire' in its alphabetical position, with the Dominions and India, in

The high tide of Imperial sentiment engendered by the war and by the conjunction of imaginative leadership here and in the Dominions was followed by the inevitable ebb. The German menace had been got rid of for good and all, it was assumed. The possibility of danger from Japan was only envisaged in Admiralty circles. The whole field of defence and foreign policy was, indeed, widely believed by public opinion in every part of the Empire to have been taken over by the League of Nations. Every government in the Commonwealth was overwhelmed by urgent domestic problems. In Canada Sir Robert Borden, carrying on the Macdonald tradition, with its equal emphasis on Canadian nationality and on effective Empire co-operation, was succeeded by Mr. Mackenzie King, with whom the stress on the former was combined with a still strong anti-Downing Street complex against any formal collective organization. In South Africa that wise statesman General Botha was to die and his brilliant and far-sighted successor, General Smuts, was to be succeeded by General Hertzog, still an avowed republican, who during the war had even attempted to secure from the Allies the restoration of the former South African republics. Presently the centrifugal, or at least negative, wing in the Commonwealth group was to be reinforced by the advent of the Irish Free State, with its long

order of their seniority, under that heading. Logically the United Kingdom should have been included with the Dominions and the failure to do so gave rise at one time to the mistaken view that 'British Empire' was intended to refer only to the United Kingdom and its colonial dependencies. In the United Nations Organization the group arrangement was dropped and each member of the Commonwealth placed alphabetically, as if to emphasize that there was no special relation between them.

tradition of racial and religious struggle against the British Government. The whole idea of a permanent Imperial Cabinet, with annual Prime Ministers' conferences and frequent meetings attended by Resident Ministers in the interval, was tacitly dropped. So was the title Imperial Cabinet, now thought to be too suggestive of the idea of a centralized system of government. Even the pre-war formal constitution of the Imperial Conference as a permanent body lapsed, and subsequent conferences tended to be regarded more as *ad hoc* reunions whose constitution and functions were left to be decided on each occasion.

In this connexion it is impossible to leave out of the picture the distraction created by the League of Nations. The structure of that body owed everything to the British precedents familiar to its architects, General Smuts, Lord Cecil, and Lord Phillimore. The League Council and Assembly were, in essence, adaptations from the Imperial War Cabinet and Conference, and the vital importance attached to the secretariat was the result of first-hand experience of Sir Maurice Hankey's work in London. How was it that the Dominion Governments were so ready to accept, not only the more elaborate organization of the League and the theoretically far more serious obligations undertaken, when they were already tending to drift away from any formal Commonwealth organization, however narrowly limited? One answer, no doubt, is to be found in the almost irresistible wave of idealist sentiment in favour of the League which swept through the British countries in the reaction after the war. Another lay in the opportunity afforded by the League to the Dominions to assert their individual international status without, in fact, incurring any serious individual responsibilities. For, to speak quite frankly, nobody in their heart of hearts took the League obligations too seriously. An Imperial Conference was a business gathering whose resolutions might lead to definite commitments, and any improvement in whose machinery might give a definite direction to the constitutional evolution of the whole Commonwealth— a matter, therefore, to be approached with circumspection and not to be lightly entrusted to subordinate Ministers. Geneva, after all, was more in the nature of a ceremonial of international goodwill where any reputable delegate could maintain both the status and the virtuous outlook of a Dominion by his presence and by the utterance of the appropriate platitudes. In the end the League shared the fate of other constitutions modelled on the outward forms of British practice without embodying its traditions and its spirit. The British Commonwealth, while apparently loosening still further the slender formal bonds which were supposed to hold it together, preserved an unbroken front in the hour of supreme peril, and displayed a power of effective action undreamt of by the outer world.

Such was the general situation when I accepted Mr. Baldwin's invitation in November 1924 to become Colonial Secretary. I did so subject to the stipulation that I must be allowed to break up the Office and create an entirely separate Office for Dominion Affairs. I had long considered that step essential in order to recognize the importance due to Dominion questions and to remove any lingering suspicion that the Dominions were still dealt with by officials accustomed to the bureaucratic control of subordinate dependencies. In this new field my first task was to address myself to that problem of the readjustment of our constitutional relations which the Imperial War Conference of 1917 had left for a special Imperial Conference to be summoned immediately after the war. This had by tacit consent been postponed, and I very soon realized that the matter would be much better handled as part of a normal Imperial Conference than by one specially convened for that purpose. In coming to this conclusion I was mainly influenced by my belief that, given the outlook of several leading Dominion Governments, the one essential condition precedent to any further advance, and, at the same time the only immediately possible step, was to get rid of every last vestige, not only of substance, but also of mere historical form, which might be thought to limit the complete independence and equality of the Dominion Governments. It was to this end that the preparatory work of the Dominions Office was for many months directed. When the Imperial Conference of 1926 met I was fortunate enough to secure the help and guidance, as chairman of the committee set up to consider Imperial relations, of Lord Balfour, whose views on the subject entirely coincided with mine.

The committee tacitly rejected from the outset any attempt to frame or even discuss any new constitutional scheme, and confined itself to the task of clarifying and defining, by common consent, the position which we had reached. If, in so doing it gave a new and fruitful direction to the subsequent course of our constitutional development, and thus became a landmark in our Imperial history, that was only in accordance with our traditions. Magna Carta, the Declaration of Rights, and other noteworthy milestones in English history, since recognized as starting-points of great developments, also professed, at the time, to be no more than explicit assertions of recognized rights. The definition of the mutual relationship between the United Kingdom and the Dominions was laid down in the following passage of our report:

'The Committee are of opinion that nothing would be gained by attempting to lay down a Constitution for the British Empire. Its widely scattered parts have very different characteristics, very different histories, and are at very different stages of evolution; while, considered as a whole, it defies classification and bears no real resemblance to any other political organization which now exists or has ever yet been tried.

'There is, however, one most important element in it which, from a strictly constitutional point of view, has now, as regards all vital matters, reached its full development— we refer to the group of self-governing communities composed of Great Britain and the Dominions. Their position and mutual relation may be readily defined. *They are autonomous communities within the British Empire, equal in status, in no way subordinate one to another in any aspect of their domestic or external affairs, though united by a common allegiance to the Crown, and freely associated as members of the British Commonwealth of Nations.*

'A foreigner endeavouring to understand the true character of the British Empire by the aid of this formula alone would be tempted to think that it was devised rather to make mutual interference impossible than to make mutual co-operation easy.

'Such a criticism, however, completely ignores the historic situation. The rapid evolution of the Oversea Dominions during the last fifty years has involved many complicated adjustments of old political machinery to changing conditions. The tendency towards equality of status was both right and inevitable. Geographical and other conditions made this impossible of attainment by the way of federation. The only alternative was by the way of autonomy; and along this road it has been steadily sought. Every self-governing member of the Empire is now the master of its destiny. In fact, if not always in form, it is subject to no compulsion whatever.

'But no account, however accurate, of the negative relations in which Great Britain and the Dominions stand to each other can do more than express a portion of the truth. The British Empire is not founded upon negations. It depends essentially, if not formally, on positive ideals. Free institutions are its life-blood. Free co-operation is its instrument. Peace, security, and progress are among its objects. Aspects of all these great themes have been discussed at the present Conference; excellent results have been thereby obtained. And, though every Dominion is now, and must always remain, the sole judge of the nature and extent of its co-operation, no common cause will, in our opinion, be thereby imperilled.

'*Equality of status, so far as Britain and the Dominions are concerned, is thus the root principle governing our Inter-Imperial Relations. But the principles of equality and similarity, appropriate to status, do not universally extent to function. Here we require something more than immutable dogmas. For example, to deal with questions of diplomacy and questions of defence, we require also flexible machinery—machinery which can, from time to time, be adapted to the changing circumstances of the world.*'

It will be noted that in the italicized sentence defining the position and mutual relations of the members of the Commonwealth the word 'Empire' is used to describe the British political organism as a whole. No other term, indeed, would be appropriate to the totality of autonomous states, dependencies, colonies, protectorates, mandated territories, feudatories, and allies which are comprehended within the orbit of our polity. Within that wider whole the relationship of certain of its members constitutes a definite political system whose character is appropriately designated by the fine old title of 'Commonwealth', a word whose use goes back to long before the days when it was peculiarly associated with the Puritan Republic. That is the correct distinction between the two words where accuracy of definition is required. But in ordinary language they are largely interchangeable, according as the emphasis is laid upon the idea of comprehensiveness and unity, or upon the ideal of free co-operation for the common weal.

One phrase, indeed, in this definition seemed to me at the time to be open to the possibility of misunderstanding. That is the phrase 'freely associated'. I urged that this might be taken to imply a right to dissociation from the Empire—as, in fact, it has been since in some quarters—but my colleagues were unanimous in holding that it could only refer to the freedom with which our association is exercised, and could have no bearing on the question of allegiance to the Crown. Freedom to break away from that allegiance may not be in dispute as a matter of practical politics, but was certainly not intended to be sanctioned by the framers of the definition, and its exercise would still be a revolutionary breach in any constitution of which the Crown is an integral part.

The defining sentence was never intended to stand alone, and when, after prolonged discussions, we had one morning agreed upon our wording, we adjourned before beginning to consider a suitable wider context in which to incorporate it. At our next meeting Lord Balfour presented us with the whole of the historic statement which I have just quoted. We duly adopted it with the change of only one unimportant word.

In the light of this covering declaration we turned to the more detailed task of dealing with such survivals of an earlier state of affairs as conflicted with it either in form or in substance. In the first category came the position of Governors-General. It was agreed that the traditional practice whereby the Governor-General was the formal official channel of communication with a Dominion Government was no longer in accordance with the constitutional position. Holding, in all essential respects, the same position in relation to public affairs in the Dominion as is held by the King in the United Kingdom, he could not, even formally, serve as agent or representative of another Government. It was decided, consequently, that all communications in future should be direct from Government to Government, the Governor-General being kept as fully informed as is the King in Great Britain of Cabinet business and public affairs. It was in the spirit of this conclusion and of the 'right of the Government of each Dominion to advise the Crown in all matters relating to its own affairs' that the appointment of Governors-General, up till then a matter of informal consultation by the Secretary of State with the Government concerned, became one entirely between that Government and the King in person.[1] It was in the same spirit that from then onwards all the Governments of the Commonwealth were regularly described as His Majesty's Governments. It was a logical consequence of the same principle, to which I have already referred in my first lecture, that such power as a Governor-General may

[1] This was explicitly affirmed in the Report of the 1930 Conference.

possess to differ from the advice of his Ministers must be exercised in his own discretion and cannot be based on any advice from a British Minister.

In the field of legislation there were certain aspects of an older state of affairs which were, in fact, purely formal. Such were the annual submission of Dominion legislation to London for the Secretary of State to intimate 'that His Majesty will not be advised to exercise his powers of disallowance', the reservation of Dominion legislation, in certain circumstances, 'for the signification of His Majesty's pleasure', and, more generally, the legal power of the Parliament at Westminster to pass legislation applicable to the Dominions. There were a few matters of substance, such as the limitation of a Dominion Parliament's legislation to its own territorial area and the Colonial Laws Validity Act of 1865 invalidating legislation by a Dominion in conflict with any legislation of the United Kingdom extending to that Dominion. We agreed that the clearing up of these points should be left to a special inter-Imperial committee of legal experts, while another expert committee should inquire into the difficult question of Merchant Shipping Registration.

Much detailed consideration was also given to the question of the procedure in connexion with treaty negotiation and international conferences, and recognition was given to the beginnings of direct diplomatic representation between the Dominions and foreign countries. All this was in line with the essentially negative though vital object of emphasizing the complete equality of the Dominions with the United Kingdom in every respect, while still maintaining the formal unity of the common Crown and the common status of

British subject which derives from it. The King's title, indeed, was reconsidered by the committee in order to bring it into line with the recognition of the Irish Free State as a Dominion, and the words 'of the United Kingdom of Great Britain and Ireland' altered to 'of Great Britain, Ireland, etc.' The only positive recommendation of the committee in regard to closer and more continuous communication was a resolution urging the 'desirability of developing a system of personal contact' at both ends, in other words of appointing United Kingdom High Commissioners in the Dominions, a logical consequence of the Governors-General ceasing to be in any sense representatives of the British Government. The conclusions of our committee were endorsed by the Conference itself, which in its final resolution summed up the whole purpose of our meeting as the promotion in all parts of the Empire of 'unity of thought and co-operation in action'.

It was in order to emphasize these words and to explain the positive, as against the purely negative, aspects of our conclusions that I spent seven months in the following year on a visit to all the Dominions, making over 300 public speeches as well as discussing many practical problems with the governments concerned. It was left for a new British Government to deal, at the Imperial Conference of 1930, with the reports of the Conferences on the Operation of Dominion Legislation and on Merchant Shipping and to prepare the necessary legislation. This was embodied, so far as the legal position was concerned, in the Statute of Westminster, which became an Act of the British Parliament in December 1931. It was accepted in full at the time by the South African and Irish Free State Parliaments, and by the Canadian Parliament with the insertion of a safeguard for the Constitution. Australia adopted Sections 2–6 of the Statute in October 1942, with effect as from 3 September 1939. New Zealand has not yet taken any similar action.

Not the least interesting and important provision of this famous statute is the declaration in the preamble that any alteration in the law touching the succession to the Throne or the Royal Style and Titles should, in order to be in accordance with the established constitutional position, require the assent of all the Dominions as well as of the United Kingdom. Significant as was its bearing on the position of the Crown as the symbol of Imperial unity, the full importance of this preamble was only realized in connexion with King Edward VIII's abdication in 1936 when, happily, no differences arose as to the course adopted. For the rest the Act explicitly lays down that the Colonial Laws Validity Act of 1865 shall not apply to the Dominions and that Dominion legislation shall not be regarded as void on the ground of repugnancy to the law of England or to any United Kingdom statute; that Dominion laws can have extra-territorial operation and that certain clauses of the Merchant Shipping Act, 1894, and of the Colonial Courts of Admiralty Act of 1890 shall not apply to the Dominions.[1] While it declares that no Act of Parliament

---

[1] Under the British Commonwealth Merchant Shipping Agreement, 1931, reciprocal arrangements were to have been made to take their place providing for the recognition of the 'common status' of a 'British ship', analogous to the common status of British subject, in whatever part of the Empire it might be registered. But no action has, in fact, been taken except by Canada, which in 1934 passed a Shipping Act repealing the Merchant Shipping Acts in so far as they were in force in Canada.

of the United Kingdom shall extend to a Dominion
unless it expressly declares that that Dominion has requested and consented to its enactment, it still leaves
intact a legal power which might on occasion prove
convenient if speedy uniform legislation were desired,
but which also covers legislation for changing the constitutions of the federal Dominions and New Zealand
which the Statute excludes from alteration except under
the conditions prevailing hitherto.

The stage in the constitutional evolution of the Commonwealth which began with Queen Victoria's Jubilee
in 1887 was rounded off half a century later at the
coronation of her great-grandson, when a new Coronation Service was adapted to the change in constitutional
relationship and a new Coronation Oath brought the
King into direct relationship with the people of each
Dominion separately mentioned.[1] The Imperial Conference which met on that occasion dealt with only one
other, but highly important, constitutional point in
affirming that the defining by more than one Dominion
of specific conditions of 'nationality' or citizenship for
its own purposes did not affect the 'common status' of
British subject, i.e. not a subject of Britain, but a subject
of the common Crown. Foreign policy and defence now
naturally preoccupied much of the attention of the conference and of the specially convened Defence Conference of 1939. On this issue it is enough to say that
practical co-operation in defence, largely in abeyance

[1] The first paragraph of the new Coronation Oath reads as follows:
'Will you solemnly promise and swear to govern the peoples of Great
Britain, Ireland, Canada, Australia, New Zealand and the Union of
South Africa, of your Possessions and the other Territories to any of
them belonging or pertaining, and of your Empire of India, according
to their respective laws and customs?'

after 1919 except to some extent, so far as Australia and New Zealand were concerned, in regard to the Singapore Base, developed steadily from about 1934 onwards and contributed greatly to the readiness of the whole Commonwealth to play its part when the world crisis came.

The economic aspect of Empire co-operation was discussed at the Imperial War Conference of 1917 and a resolution passed urging the granting of preferences wherever customs duties were imposed. This was followed up by the British Government in the budget of 1919 by preferential remissions on the existing duties on dried fruits, sugar, tobacco, wine and spirits, as well as on the McKenna duties, and was reciprocated by substantial increases in Dominion preferences in the next few years. The Imperial Economic Conference of 1923 resulted in the British Government undertaking a further substantial extension of this remission, though again within the limits of its existing tariff. This undertaking was reversed by Mr. Snowden in the following year. When the Conservative Government was again returned at the end of 1924 Mr. Baldwin felt that he was precluded from a direct fulfilment of the promise made by his Government the year before, but I was able to secure Cabinet agreement to allotting the monetary equivalent of the promised preferences to assisting the marketing of Empire produce in this country. The administration of this fund was entrusted to the Secretary of State for Dominion Affairs as Chairman of an Empire Marketing Board on which various other Ministers, Dominion and Colonial representatives, as well as individual specialists on publicity and other subjects were represented in an advisory capacity.

Conceived as a makeshift way of honouring a pledge which could not conveniently be fulfilled in its original form, the Empire Marketing Board was destined in the seven short years of its life to prove the most fruitful and original mechanism for the stimulation of Imperial economic development and co-operation that had yet been devised. It developed, on very original lines, the whole conception of publicity for the idea of 'buying Empire', and so paved the way most effectively for the policy afterwards officially adopted at Ottawa. More important still, it gave an immense stimulus to research of all kinds in connexion with the production, carriage, storage, and marketing of Empire products, both by generous grants to existing institutions and the creation of new institutions, and by promoting personal intercourse between research workers in all parts of the Empire. Of no less immediate and practical value was its work in connexion with statistical and other economic investigations and market intelligence as well as in the actual promotion of individual marketing schemes. Any adequate account of all its varied activities would fill a volume. For my present purpose it is sufficient to say that the Empire Marketing Board gave a new life and colour to the whole conception of Empire economic unity, and to pay my tribute of gratitude and admiration to Sir Stephen Tallents, its ever resourceful secretary, and to the band of enthusiastic colleagues and fellow workers whom we got together.

After the Ottawa Conference the British Government took the line that, having now fulfilled the original promises of 1923, it would no longer maintain the Empire Marketing Fund unless the Dominions were prepared there and then to agree to a scheme based on all-round contributions. The whole fruitful scheme was whittled down to a timid little project for a fund of £24,000 a year, to be jointly contributed by the whole Empire, to cover the existing cost of the Imperial Economic Committee and of some of the market intelligence work previously carried on by the Empire Marketing Board, of the Imperial Shipping Committee, and of the headquarters of the existing Imperial Agricultural Bureaux.

At the 1930 Imperial Conference, with the shadow of world economic depression already impending, the Dominions, led by Mr. (now Viscount) Bennett, who had succeeded Mr. Mackenzie King as Prime Minister of Canada, once more returned to the charge on the whole subject of Imperial Preference, only to be as categorically rebuffed by Mr. Snowden as they had been by Mr. Asquith in 1907. Within a year the world economic crisis forced a complete reconsideration of British economic policy and the adoption of an all-round scheme of moderate protection. With this as a basis it was possible at the Ottawa Conference of 1932 to frame a substantial scheme of mutual preference embodied in a dozen bilateral agreements. The result of the wide expansion of profitable mutual trade thus secured, helped in the monetary sphere by the liberation of sterling from the restrictive influence of the gold standard, was to enable the British Empire to make a more rapid recovery from the world depression than any other group of countries. A remarkable expansion of inter-Imperial trade was accompanied by a relatively smaller but still also marked expansion of the external trade of the Empire which could not have taken place if, in the absence of the Ottawa agreements, each part of the Empire had been forced to pursue a narrowly autarkic policy. Unfortunately, owing largely to the particular composition of the British Government of the day, the Ottawa agreements were defended here mainly on the ground of their merits as trade bargains. Their constitutional significance as an essential part of any effective policy of Commonwealth co-operation was never sufficiently emphasized.

Be that as it may, the final and full justification of twenty years of development in Imperial relations in every field was afforded by the outbreak of war in 1939. It was in accordance with that development that the declaration of war was decided on separately by each Parliament. The decision of Eire to remain neutral only marked the absence of that unity of thought leading to co-operation in action which was still, for the time being, characteristic of her peculiar outlook. While nothing could have been more magnificent than the actual unity in effort and sacrifice displayed by the whole Empire in that supreme struggle, it cannot, however, be said that, on the purely constitutional side, quite the same advantage was taken of the situation as it was by the vision and statesmanship of the Empire leaders of the First World War.

An Australian request for the setting up of an Imperial War Cabinet in 1940 came to nothing, as the Prime Ministers of some other Dominions did not see their way to coming over at the time. A renewed suggestion by Australia in 1941 that an 'Accredited Representative' of Australia should attend when matters of general interest were under discussion was at once agreed to, but besides Australia only India and (on a few occasions) New Zealand availed themselves of the opportunity, both at the time and again in 1945. There were, however, two important 'Prime Ministers' Meetings' in 1944 and again in 1945 on the eve of the San Francisco United Nations Conference, as well as a Telecommunications Conference in the latter year. On the other hand, aviation enabled many more individual meetings between Empire Prime Ministers to take place here and overseas. Not a few memorable addresses to Parliament and to wider gatherings were given by Dominion statesmen while Mr. Churchill's informal conference with the Canadian Cabinet in 1943 furnished a further interesting precedent. Moreover, the Dominion Governments were kept in the closest touch with general policy by regular daily meetings of the High Commissioners with the Dominions Secretary. It may, indeed, be said that, in spite of the obvious distaste of certain Empire Governments for anything savouring of formal constitutional unity, thoroughly effective contact and co-operation were maintained so far as the conduct of the war was concerned.

On the economic side, indeed, so far from any positive methods of more effective co-operation being studied, the British Government felt constrained under insistent American pressure to contemplate the reduction, if not the elimination, of Imperial Preference as part of the Lend-Lease Agreement of 1942, and used its influence with the Dominions in the same direction. Neither then, nor in connexion with the pledges subsequently given in connexion with the Washington Loan Agreements, does there seem to have been any attempt to assert, in the face of American dictation, the constitutional aspect of the principle of Empire co-operation established, after a generation of controversy, at Ottawa.

Nevertheless it looks as if we are entering upon a

period in world affairs in which the desirability of improving the machinery, political and economic, of Commonwealth co-operation may well appeal increasingly to all concerned. The economic situation everywhere is not likely to make possible the fulfilment, either by Empire or by foreign countries, not to speak of avowed opponents like the Soviet group, of the American policy of restoring the economic individualist internationalism of the last century. There are few illusions this time as to the millennium of universal peace being already in sight. If the League of Nations collapsed, after some sixteen years of more or less hopeful existence, so soon as it was brought up against a serious conflict of ideological and power policies, the United Nations Organization begins with that conflict in undisguised and blatant intensity and would seem to be less likely to promote peace than to divide the world into two hostile extremist camps. The British nations, committed to neither extreme in economic or political theory, may before long come to the conclusion that they can best preserve their own peace, and live their own lives in their own way, by closer co-operation both in the mutual promotion of their welfare and in relation to the outside world.

If so they are not likely to depart in any way from the main principle of free and equal co-operation between nations as nations—the Commonwealth principle I would call it—in favour of any centralizing or mechanical structure of a federal or quasi-federal character. The argument for federalism, supported at one time by the able writers of the *Round Table* group and with almost prophetic fervour by Mr. Lionel Curtis, is based on certain assumptions which bear little relation to actual present-day conditions and are inconsistent with the whole character and tradition of our constitutional system. One is that the functions of government can be clearly divided between those wider functions which concern the external life of the State, and are, therefore, naturally assigned to the federal power, and the narrower more domestic functions which can be left to the subordinate units. The whole course of political and economic evolution has tended to obliterate that division. Foreign affairs, defence, monetary, industrial, commercial, transport, and social policy have become an indissoluble complex of national life. No nation conscious of its national existence is prepared to surrender any of these functions to an outside authority. Nor would that outside authority be efficient for its own purposes if it were confined to a few selected functions; if, say, it controlled defence, but had no say in the development of the great basic munition industries or in merchant shipping or civil aviation. The system of the Commonwealth, the system of co-operation between nations as nations, is not merely the only one that the Dominions—or for that matter this country—would look at, but is one that covers the whole field of national activities whether conducive to security or to welfare in the widest sense, to the good life in peace or to victory in war.

Another assumption underlying the federal case is that government must rest upon some ultimate basis of sovereignty and must, in a democratic age, be government by delegation from an electorate, at any rate in respect of functions to be exercised in common. There is no warrant for this, as I have shown earlier, in our British constitutional system which knows of no ultimate sovereignty, but is based on government from above subject to popular consent, the two balanced and harmonized in Parliament. The natural and obvious way of securing efficient unity in action under our system is for the Governments of our common Crown to agree, and then to secure for that agreement the assent of their peoples through their Parliaments. It is a method which, incidentally, disposes of the almost insoluble problem of how to allocate voting power in an Imperial Federation. In any case the federal argument assumes throughout that what creates efficiency in action is the mechanical unity of structure and not the underlying unity of thought and purpose. It is the same error as that which makes some simple-minded people believe that the United Nations Organization will be more effective to maintain peace than the League of Nations because it has 'got teeth in it', i.e. contemplates more definite coercive action—on paper.

Within the limits of the Commonwealth principle there are at any rate certain obvious methods of securing greater efficiency in co-operation. One is to resume where we left off at the end of the First World War and once more make the Imperial Conference a permanent institution with regular annual meetings of its chief representatives and subsidiary meetings in between. The development of aviation has made it far easier than it was twenty-five years ago for Prime Ministers to manage to attend more frequently than in the past. On the other hand, the development of wireless telephony has made it possible for a Prime Minister, if unable to attend himself, to keep in continuous intimate touch with and in control of any colleague whom he may depute to represent him.

Such a regularized system of meetings would naturally necessitate a secretarial staff belonging to the Imperial Conference as a whole, and at the disposal of all its members. So long as conference arrangements are still supposed to be the business of the United Kingdom Government, an atmosphere of constraint and hesitation is bound to surround all the proceedings. There may be nominal equality of status, but there is always a certain feeling on the part of the Dominions that they are being managed, with a consequent timidity on the British side about any action that might lend justification to that feeling. This does not make for businesslike procedure either in preparing agenda or in seeing that conclusions when adopted are, in fact, followed up. It is on the economic side, in particular, that the need for a clearing-house for information, for preparation of materials, for preliminary discussions and subsequent working out of details, and of a staff at all times available for these purposes, is most obvious.

Considerations of practical convenience naturally indicate this country as the appropriate centre for any permanent Conference Secretariat. But it is impossible to ignore the psychological objections to placing a body which should be equally at the disposal of all the partners in the Commonwealth in immediate and continuous contact with the administrative machinery of the most powerful and experienced partner. There would have been no agreement upon any permanent League of Nations Secretariat if it had been suggested that it should be established in Downing Street or next door to the Quai d'Orsay. It is at any rate worth considering, when the need for the creation of an Imperial Conference Secretariat becomes sufficiently recognized, whether its inception would not be facilitated and its usefulness enhanced by making its headquarters away from London. If so, then no more appropriate centre could be suggested, in view of the Imperial character of the Crown, than within the precincts of a royal residence such as Windsor or Hampton Court.

I say sufficiently recognized, for at present there still exists in some quarters that curious survival of an older anti-Downing Street complex which shrinks, as between Commonwealth countries, from the ordinary machinery, not for framing policy, but purely for more effective inter-communication and dispatch of business, which is accepted as natural and inevitable in the case, not only of the United Nations, but of a regional association like the Pan American Union.[1] With it goes a corresponding dislike of the adjective 'Imperial', which has recently gone to the extent of leading the British Government in its latest defence reorganization to drop the adjective from the designation of the Committee of Imperial Defence. That body has, of course, never been a collectively organized Imperial Committee of Defence though Dominion representatives have regularly attended it when their part in the broad problems of Empire defence have come under consideration. But its subject matter has been, and must always be, Imperial Defence and the abandonment of the title would seem to have been an illogical as well as weak concession to an attitude which seems to me out of date both in relation

[1] The suggestion for a Commonwealth Secretariat which was put forward in 1943 by Mr. Curtin, on behalf of Australia, was publicly deprecated by Mr. Mackenzie King. The 1944 Prime Ministers' Meeting showed that no progress in that direction was feasible for the time being.

to the evolution of the Commonwealth and to the present and prospective state of the world.

While some such central clearing-house is, to my mind, the next really important step forward in the organization of co-operation, progress in the near future is likely to pursue empirical lines. Mutual contact will be increasingly developed through the High Commissioners at both ends as the several governments realize the practical advantages of extending the scope and authority of men whom they can both trust and now effectively control. This method of contact, now adopted by the United Kingdom Government in all the Dominions, will no doubt be further extended to inter-Dominion communications. Standing committees and research organizations of all kinds will be formed as the practical need for them is felt, and will be joined, in the first instance, by those most conscious of the need. The practice of holding official and unofficial Empire conferences on every kind of subject, scientific, technical, commercial, will spread. Such conferences of specialists are generally much more Imperial in their outlook, inspired as they are by the greatness of the field which the Empire offers for the development of their subject, than conferences of governments, naturally jealously watchful of their individual status and interests. There is scope for independent bodies under Royal Charter, enjoying both government and private support. A striking example of the success of such an independent inter-Imperial institution is the War Graves Commission. Another, with a history going back to the Ottawa Conference of 1894, is the Imperial and International Wireless and Cable Organization which was created in 1928 upon the

foundation of the old Pacific Cable Board and has now
again been reorganized. Besides these one might men-
tion the Imperial Economic Committee, the Imperial
Shipping Committee, and the Executive Council of the
Imperial Agricultural Bureaux.[1]

It has frequently been suggested that the constitution
of the Imperial Conference itself should be altered by
including representatives of all parties from each Parliament of the Empire. Such a change, it is argued, would
give greater authority to its conclusions and insure continuity in their execution. But it has never been favoured
by Dominion Governments. Nor is it really appropriate
to the constitution of a body which is primarily a conference of governments. A possible way of meeting the
need underlying the suggestion would be, not to alter
the constitution of the conference itself, but to encourage
the meeting, outside the conference, of all-party delegations from each of the Parliaments. Such an assemblage,
while possessing no legislative authority, might serve the
conference as a means of testing parliamentary opinion
on issues involving legislation or finance, before coming
to conclusions, and of insuring more responsible parliamentary support afterwards. The great success of the
Empire Parliamentary Association in the last thirty-five
years in bringing members of the Parliaments of the
Empire into personal contact, and in encouraging
informal discussions between them, encourages the
hope that such meetings of regularly constituted parliamentary delegations would be a useful development

[1] This supervises the following bodies: The Imperial Bureaux of Soil
Science, of Animal Health, of Animal Nutrition, of Animal Genetics,
of Plant Genetics (one for herbage plants and one for other crops), of
Fruit Production, of Forestry, of Dairy Science and of Agricultural
Parasitology, and the Entomological and Mycological Institutes.

of the whole conception of independent co-operation through intimate contact. It would be essentially in line with that conception of the nature of the British and Dominion Constitutions which I have throughout endeavoured to stress.

In any case, whatever improvements in actual detailed methods of co-operation may yet be worked out, the essential constitutional principles on which the British or Britannic[1] Commonwealth is based now stand out clearly. The starting-point of its evolution, the keystone of the constitutional arch, 'the symbol of our partnership and the focus of our common loyalty', to quote Mr. Baldwin's words at the Coronation Conference of 1937, has been the Crown. The part which the Crown has played in the evolution of our constitutional system at home, the peculiar character which it has given to the actual working of that system in practice, and the unique position to which the Monarchy itself, as distinct from the Crown as an institution, has attained, have all had their corresponding influence,

---

[1] The whole question of terminology in our Imperial affairs is not without its difficulties, arising from the very fact that we have evolved from a centralized Empire to a decentralized one. The adjective 'British' has to do double duty for that which pertains to the United Kingdom and that which pertains to the Empire as a whole, just as the Union Jack does double duty as our local flag here and as the common flag of the Empire. There is a real disadvantage in this in so far as it tends to preserve an unconsciously centralist outlook on Empire affairs in the mind of the public here, and to foster a corresponding anti-Imperial complex in other parts of the Empire. We may, perhaps, some day accept the distinction suggested by that pioneer of progressive thinking on Empire questions, Mr. Richard Jebb, and use 'Britannic' for Imperial, reserving 'British' for more strictly local purposes, just as we may some day make up our minds to distinguish officially between a United Kingdom flag and a common Imperial flag. Or we may just rub along as we are, avoiding any change that is not actually forced upon us.

not only upon the constitutional tradition of each part of the Empire separately, but upon the development of the Commonwealth and Empire as a whole.

The same process of differentiation which, in each country, has enabled the Monarch to embody the unity and continuity of the national life, and to become the focus of all those loyalties which transcend the conflicts of the hour, has equally made it natural that he should, for the whole Empire, become the embodiment of a wider patriotism, the object of a loyalty transcending more immediate loyalties. For in each case it has enabled that higher, spiritual function of the Crown to be developed without prejudice to the fullest freedom in the conduct of governments, whether pursuing separate party policies within a nation, or separate national policies within the Empire. Moreover, that function is one which can make its appeal across the medium of every kind of political outlook. Loyalty to the Throne is a common bond, however differently conceived, between the most constitutionally developed and the most primitive of His Majesty's subjects. No other satisfactory common centre and apex, indeed, could well be conceived for so complex and varied a system of governments and communities as ours.

Human nature not only craves for symbols but prefers them personal and human. The Monarch's domestic life typifies not only the majesty of the State but also the intimacy of ordinary human events. Births and deaths, marriage and parenthood, sickness and recovery: the interest in these happenings helps to unite the whole of the King's subjects in a common family feeling. This personal and human aspect of royalty has been enormously enhanced by the discoveries of science. Modern methods of transport have made the personality of our King and Queen a household recollection in every part of the Empire. Every ceremonial event in which royalty takes part is reproduced, not only in print, but visibly and audibly for every British subject. On the occasion of the Coronation, not only the swelling music of the Abbey, but every word of the Archbishop's address, every response of the royal pair, were heard more clearly in the farthest parts of the Empire than by many of those present at the actual service. Not only on great ceremonial occasions but on every Christmas Day the King's own words of goodwill to his peoples, to his wider family, are heard in countless homes all round the world; by the lonely miner in the Canadian Arctic, the pioneer in the Australian bush, the village headman in India and the sailor at sea. A distant symbol has become an intimate presence, quickening in a unique fashion in countless individuals scattered over the many lands and seas the sense of a personal link binding them together.

The differentiation between the personal aspect of the Monarchy and the Crown as a political institution has, however, never been a divorce. There is under our system no such thing as a definite separation between Monarchy and Crown, no mere personal union of separate Crowns, such as once linked Hanover to England or Austria to Hungary. It is the same common Crown which is an integral part of the constitution of each part of the whole Empire, as is clearly emphasized in the preamble to the Statute of Westminster. This gives to the whole Commonwealth a constitutionally indissoluble unity which is as essential a part of its constitution as the absolute independence and equality of its several partners. The fact that, in practice, any Dominion, or for that matter the United Kingdom, might disclaim all further connexion with or responsibility for the rest, and emphasize that decision by declaring itself a republic,[1] without forcible interference, would not affect the fundamentally unconstitutional nature of such a step.

Constitutionally and legally the British Empire, while in one aspect comprising a variety of governments, many of which work in complete independence and subject to no external authority, is also, in another aspect, one single, indissoluble body corporate composed of the King and his subjects. This latter aspect, naturally less discussed in the constitutional readjustment of recent years, still holds good and colours all the relationships of Empire. As subjects of the King, all inhabitants of the Empire owe loyalty not only to the King, but, in virtue of their loyalty to him, to each other. All the Parliaments of the Empire are Parliaments in which the same Crown is an integral part, and members who have sworn the oath of allegiance[2] to that Crown have always to bear in mind not only their immediate obligation towards their own constituents, but the obligation of reconciling the interests of those constituents with the wider interests of all their fellow subjects under the Crown. His Majesty's Ministers of the different governments of the Empire are all fellow-servants of the same Crown, and, as such, in a very real sense, colleagues, as is well understood by any of us who

---

[1] It is the repudiation of mutual responsibility and the rejection of the 'common status' of subject of the Crown that would constitute the real test of separation, not the mere description of a constitution as republican.

[2] In the case of Eire this obligation was removed by the Constitution (Removal of Oath) Bill, 1932, contrary to Article 4 of the Treaty of 1921.

have ever taken part in an Imperial Conference. That obligation of mutual support and co-operation which flows from the fact of a common Crown constitutes, so to speak, the Common Law of the Empire—a Common Law which is enforced, not by any central authority, but by the free action of all the governments and peoples that live under the Crown.

As in our domestic constitution so, too, in that of the Commonwealth the secret of its working lies in the sense of responsibility. In the one case it is responsibility for the unity and stability of the national life, in the other for the maintenance and development of our whole Imperial heritage. That this sense of Imperial responsibility is not yet fully or equally developed everywhere in the Commonwealth must be admitted. Time is required in order to enable the new conception of our mutual relations to be fully understood. The old conception of the British Empire as a planetary system with this country as the central sun, the old suspicion, dating from colonial days, of Downing Street control and interference, have not yet wholly faded out. We are only gradually beginning to realize, here and in the Dominions, that the Empire is not an external bond, a super-state limiting our national lives, but, like the Kingdom of Heaven, within us. It is not something to which we submit, that owns us: it is something that we all own, an enlargement and exaltation of our own national and individual lives. Imperial unity is inherent in our constitutions and not imposed by a federal constitution from without—inherent in a common Crown, in a sense of responsibility for the common interest springing from that common focus, and strengthened by innumerable strands of common interest, kindred thought, and mutual sympathy.

So, too, it will take time for the Dominions to appreciate fully that the status to which they have attained is not a mere national but an Imperial status. They have been gladly welcomed by Britain to equality with herself, no common, ordinary nation, with a precarious, limited, nominal independence, and a narrow, introverted vision, but a great Imperial nation, proud of her achievement, still confident in her strength, still unafraid of great responsibilities, with a temper generous as the breadth of her horizon. They can only realize gradually how superior, in status and dignity, as well as in practical convenience, is their position as compared with that of most of the so-called independent nations of the world outside. They enjoy every liberty, every privilege enjoyed by the ordinary run of sovereign states. But they enjoy much more. Within the circle of the Commonwealth they can count on the co-operation, the support, in peace and war, of their partner states, as well as on the privileges of an almost world-wide citizenship for every one of their citizens. There is no nation now outside the Commonwealth whose status, whose dignity, whose power and security would not be enhanced by admission to such a partnership. There is none now within the Commonwealth that would not lose immeasurably in every sense, above all in freedom of action and in spiritual growth, in severance from its association.

It is no less necessary for us in this country to realize that our Imperial status has not been diminished by recent constitutional changes. It is sometimes said, and in one sense correctly, that we are now only one of the Dominions. But we are still the senior of the Imperial nations, with the most highly developed sense of a common Imperial responsibility. That responsibility has not been lessened by the admission of equal partners who can join us in the task of fulfilling it more successfully. It is still for us to give leadership to the whole Empire, if that leadership is in us, and if we can win it on our freely recognized merit and not on any obsolete claim to supremacy or even primacy. And we still have immediate responsibilities, in relation to foreign affairs, to defence, to India, to the Colonial Empire, so definitely and predominantly ours that we could not, in respect of them, abdicate our leadership if we wished.

It would take me far beyond the scope of these lectures if I attempted to deal with the specific constitutional issue in India. So far, at any rate, as India's position in the Commonwealth and *vis-à-vis* the world is concerned, it has already for all practical purposes been assimilated to that of the Dominions. She is represented at all Imperial Conferences and on the United Nations Organization on the same footing as Canada or Australia, through representatives chosen by the Viceroy in Council. That council, whose majority view the Viceroy is normally by law obliged to accept, has for some years had a substantial Indian majority. It is to-day entirely composed of Indian political leaders chosen by the chiefs of the two main organized parties. The new Indian Government operates, it is true, within the present constitution as laid down in the India Acts of 1919 and 1935. But that has already, in fact, been expanded to cover the whole field of external policy and defence. There remains the problem of agreement upon a future Indian Constitution and the practical right, conceded in advance, for the framers of that constitution, to opt for severance of the Commonwealth connexion.

We can only hope that, by the time that question arises in a definite form, the experience of freedom and responsibility now enjoyed will present the advantages of maintaining that connexion in a very different light from that in which it has appeared to Indian political leaders in the past.[1]

There remain innumerable problems within the wider orbit of the Empire outside the present limits of the Commonwealth which only the future can solve. That some day the term 'Commonwealth' shall in effect cover the whole Empire is an ideal which will need many stages for its realization. Burma, indeed, is already well on the way towards Dominion status, and Southern Rhodesia, whether by itself or under some form of closer union with Northern Rhodesia and Nyasaland, has long been on the outer fringe of the Commonwealth circle. It may well be that the next stage in the evolution of the dependent Empire will take the shape of a series of regional groupings, in some cases in closer association with particular Dominions. This has already been clearly envisaged in post-war discussions on defence,

[1] Since 15 August 1947 British India has been divided into two Dominions, India and Pakistan. For the time being, at any rate, both Dominions retain the Commonwealth relationship, not only with the rest of the British Commonwealth, but with each other. Their citizenship is not mutually exclusive and it is to be hoped that, whether they stay in the wider Commonwealth or not, they will maintain the Commonwealth relationship among themselves as the basis of increasing Indian unity both for defence and for economic development. Their present constitutions are provisional, the constituent assemblies chosen by the provincial legislatures also acting as temporary parliaments. India has kept Earl Mountbatten as its first Governor-General. Mr. Jinnah has become the first Governor-General of Pakistan, thus merging the functions of the Crown and those of the dominant party leader in a single individual. With the exception of Hyderabad the Indian States would seem to have decided to accede to one or other of the two Dominions for the limited purposes of foreign policy, defence, and communications.

and will, no doubt, also find its application in the economic field. A South-East Asiatic group, including Burma, Ceylon, and the Malayan colonies; an East African group closely associated with the Rhodesias and the South African Union; a West Indian group linked with Canada—these and other possibilities naturally occur to one. The countries of the Middle Eastern region, too, though not within the British Imperial system, seem destined to remain closely associated with it in this shrinking world.

It is, indeed, in relation to the whole problem of world organization that our experiment in unity through free co-operation may be of greatest value. I have not concealed my view that I regard the United Nations Organization, because of the incompatibility of the ideals and outlook of its members, to be, at this stage, more likely to endanger peace than to promote it. I would even go further and say that in the present state of the world any organization which attempts to cover the world as a whole is bound to be either ineffective or mischievous unless it confines itself within very modest limits as a meeting-place and standing conference, and avoids all idea of claiming any executive or coercive power.

If I am right in believing that it is not paper constitutions, but only unity of thought and purpose which can create unity of action, then clearly the only international association that is likely to be fruitful is one of like-minded nations. That like-mindedness may be based on history or on race, on political ideology or on geography, or on a combination of some or all of these. It is in that direction that, I believe, lies the best hope of progress towards peace and prosperity in the world. It means following the natural line of evolution from the smaller unit to the greater which considerations of defence and of economic prosperity alike demand under modern conditions. It means the creation of new broader patriotisms which may help to solve problems insoluble hitherto, bringing true peace and co-operation where peace to-day is most endangered and co-operation most to seek. That is the need of our generation, and it is in that direction, towards the emergence of regional or ideological groupings, that the world seems, in fact, already to be trending.

If that is the right line of approach then, for the reasons which I have already given, I doubt whether actual federation will provide a feasible method by which independent nations, highly conscious of their national individuality, can be brought together in effective co-operation. On the other hand, the principle of the Commonwealth, the principle of free co-operation over the whole field of national life, inspired by common ideals, standards of conduct and political methods, as well as by common material interests, would seem to be far more appropriate. We have, in our long history, again and again been pioneers in constitutional and economic thought and method. Our example, sometimes, indeed, imperfectly understood, has often been an inspiration to other nations in looking for a solution of their own problems. It may well be that to the peoples of our sorely vexed neighbour continent of Europe, as well as to other world regions, the latest achievement, incomplete as it is, of the British political genius may afford at least a clue worth following up in their efforts to repair their shattered existence and to build up a happier future. If so, we shall have builded even better than we knew.

V

POSTSCRIPT 1953

THE six years which have passed since this little
volume was first published have witnessed some
important changes in the flexible constitution of the
United Kingdom. Even more important has been the
evolution—in many respects a transformation—of that
Commonwealth which General Smuts once described
in prescient terms as 'a dynamic, evolving system,
always going forward to new destinies.[1] Some brief
account of these changes has become necessary, not
only to bring the position up to date but also to
illustrate the inherent principles which the latest phases
of our constitutional development have followed.

The *de facto* freedom of any member nation to sever
its connexion with the Commonwealth has long been
accepted as a matter of practical politics. But it was
not asserted as a constitutional right by the Imperial
Conference of 1926,[2] and was first claimed as such by
the South African Parliament in a reservation to its
approval of the Report of the Conference on the
Operation of Dominion Legislation of 1929. This was
brought before the Imperial Conference of 1930 by
General Hertzog, and noted without discussion. It was,
however, treated as inherent in Dominion status in the
British Government's offer to India in 1942, and has
since been generally recognized as a matter of constitutional principle, if not of strict constitutional law.

[1] Address to both Houses of Parliament, 15 May 1917.
[2] See page 131 for the meaning of 'freely associated' in the sentence
defining the nature of the Commonwealth.

When the Burmese National Convention opted for secession in 1947 Mr. Attlee, in moving the Second Reading of the Burma Independence Bill, expressed his Government's view as follows:

'In our view, nations have the right to decide on the nature of their own government. The British Commonwealth of Nations is a free association of peoples, not a collection of subject nations. When therefore, after due consideration, the elected representatives of the people of Burma chose independence, it was, I believe, the duty of His Majesty's Government to take the necessary steps to implement their decision.'

It is worth noting that the Acts passed in the same year in respect of Ceylon, India, and Pakistan were also 'Independence Acts', thus emphasizing the fact that a Dominion was not regarded as less independent than a foreign state. In 1949 Eire put the final touch to the whittling away of all connexion with the Commonwealth by repealing the External Relations Act of 1936 and declaring itself a republic. The Ireland Act, passed by the parliament of the United Kingdom in 1949, while recognizing the Republic of Ireland, declared it not to be 'a foreign country for the purpose of any law in force' in the United Kingdom and its Colonies, Protectorates or Trust Territories, a principle already embodied in the treatment of Irish citizens in this country under the British Nationality Act of 1948. In this and other respects administrative convenience, and a certain refusal to treat Irish behaviour seriously, prevailed over the logical conclusion from a step which could only deepen and make more permanent the rift between Eire and Northern Ireland. At the same time the Act affirmed that 'in no event will Northern Ireland cease to be part of His Majesty's Dominions and of the United Kingdom without the consent of the Parliament of Northern Ireland'.

A far more important issue, affecting the very nature of the Commonwealth, was raised when, subsequent to the setting up of India and Pakistan as two separate Dominions in 1947, the Indian Constituent Assembly declared that India was to become a sovereign independent Republic. In bringing this before the Conference of Commonwealth Governments in April 1949 the Indian Government at the same time expressed the desire of India to remain a member of the Commonwealth. In the defining sentence of the 1926 Conference the self-governing communities within the British Empire were described as 'united by a common allegiance to the Crown, *and* freely associated as members of the British Commonwealth of Nations'. Were the older nations of the Commonwealth, in fact, prepared to agree that voluntary association, without the underlying legal unity implied in a common allegiance, might be a sufficient bond of unity? In other words, to allow *and* to be read as *or*? Refusal meant the end of a historic connexion which India still valued, and in which the others, and, above all, this country, felt a legitimate pride. It would also mean the end of the great experiment of a Commonwealth based on the equal association of nations of wholly different racial origins and historic and religious traditions. It was a difficult decision which many serious thinkers felt might involve the weakening of a real unity for an illusory compromise, sacrificing such substance as the Commonwealth still possessed for a verbal shadow.

After no little searching of heart the Conference agreed to meet India's request. India, for her part, accepted the King 'as the symbol of the free association of the independent member nations and, as such, the Head of the Commonwealth', while the other Governments accepted and recognized India's continuing membership of the Commonwealth, at the same time putting it on record that their own constitutional position was not thereby changed. It was a conclusion based on a frank recognition of the fact that the deep emotional and historic associations which have linked the Crown with the lives of the older members might not be shared by nations with a very different past, and on the conviction that free association and co-operation had become the real binding element in Commonwealth unity. At the same time the function of the Crown as the symbol of unity was recognized as existing in its own intrinsic psychological quality independently of its legal and constitutional origins. Only the event can prove or disprove the wisdom of the decision taken. It was a great act of faith in the dynamic strength of freedom. Such acts of faith have more than once been justified in our history.

In its immediate practical aspects co-operation has not been affected. The Indian Constitution has followed the British type of parliamentary responsible government, and an Indian Prime Minister at a Commonwealth Conference is in the same position as a British or Australian Prime Minister, normally able to implement any conclusions with which he may concur. But some new constitutional problems may arise with regard to the actual membership of the Commonwealth. General consent was obviously required for the acceptance of an Indian Republic as a full and equal member of a Commonwealth hitherto based on allegiance to a common Crown. But how far has the Commonwealth, like the United Nations, become a corporate body whose assent is required for the admission of any new member of whatever origin? There is nothing in the new constitutional structure of the Commonwealth to prevent a foreign nation, whether monarchy or republic, wishing to join it. In that case admission would, no doubt, have to be subject to the approval of the existing partners. But does that apply equally to a community of British subjects which has attained to complete self-government? In other words could the United Kingdom Government, by conceding complete autonomy to the Gold Coast, secure its automatic admission as a partner in the Commonwealth? In answer to a question on this point the Secretary of State for Commonwealth Relations on 7 June 1951 made it clear that, in view of the interest of other Commonwealth Governments in constitutional developments in the Colonial Empire, it was the 'practice to inform them of major developments in that sphere', and that, 'following past practice', all existing members would be consulted on any question of admission to full and independent membership, 'which is, of course, a matter for all members of the Commonwealth'. It may be presumed that, when the case arises, it will be decided, again in accordance with Commonwealth practice, by general agreement and not as the result of any formal vote.

The way had, in a sense, been paved for the change in the structure of the Commonwealth involved in the admission to membership of a republic, by the change in the nature of the status of British subject introduced by the Canadian Citizenship Act of 1946, and followed by the British Nationality Act of 1948 and by similar legislation in other Commonwealth countries. Before this the status of British subject was defined in identical terms in all Commonwealth countries. Certain privileges of national citizenship were further defined and confined by national legislation in certain countries. But, broadly speaking, the basic foundation, both within the Commonwealth and in relation to the outside world, was the 'common status' of British subject, and I was still justified in saying in 1946 that in one aspect the British Empire was 'one single, indissoluble body corporate composed of the King and his subjects' (see page 152).

The Canadian Act inverted the position by first defining Canadian citizenship, making the status of British subject consequential upon it, and then recognizing as British subjects in Canada persons who were British subjects under the law of the part of the Commonwealth to which they belonged. The United Kingdom Government decided to follow suit, considering that, apart from the desirability of consistency between the laws of the Commonwealth on so important a matter, the Canadian principle offered certain administrative advantages. A Commonwealth conference of experts was convened, and on the strength of their report, which, however, has never been published, the Government carried the British Nationality Act 1948. This created a new citizenship of the United Kingdom and Colonies which, like the citizenship of the other Commonwealth countries, automatically confers the status of British subject, with the alternative designation 'Commonwealth citizen', on the citizens of other Commonwealth countries. These can now only become citizens of the United Kingdom and Colonies on registration at the end of a year. In other words a South African or Australian must, in theory, wait a year for a citizenship here which is automatically enjoyed by a Basuto or Fijian. In practice, however, there has been no departure from the long established policy whereby all British subjects or Commonwealth citizens enjoy the same rights in the United Kingdom irrespective of their particular citizenship.

In other Commonwealth countries the differentiation is, in varying degrees, much more marked, the difference between the status of British subject and that of an alien being in some cases whittled down to a minimum. In South Africa, for instance, national citizenship can only be acquired by a British subject after five years (as against six for an alien) and even then at the discretion of a Minister. India, Pakistan, and Ceylon give no reciprocal citizen rights, so far as voting is concerned. The practical result has been the substitution, for an all-embracing underlying citizenship, of a system of varying preferential mutual concessions differentiating a Commonwealth citizen from an alien both generally and in respect of the attainment of citizen rights. These latter are now, in large measure, mutually exclusive. So far as Canada, Australia, South Africa, and Ceylon, but not New Zealand and Southern Rhodesia, are concerned, acquisition of United Kingdom citizenship by registration terminates national citizenship. A Canadian who returns to his own country after registering as a United

Kingdom or Australian citizen, is now no longer a Canadian citizen. It is difficult to see what administrative advantages in thus emphasizing the separate nationality of the various members of the Commonwealth were held to outweigh the impairment to individuals of what used to be regarded as one of the most valuable privileges of membership of the Commonwealth.

On the other hand the new principle has, no doubt, made it easier to extend these concessions to Commonwealth citizens who, like citizens of the Indian Republic, do not regard themselves as British subjects, and even to citizens of the Irish Republic who are not Commonwealth citizens. It thus, as I have suggested, paved the way to the retention of India in the Commonwealth, and may, at some future date, facilitate the adhesion to the Commonwealth of states now outside it. It might also permit, on the Irish model, of special preferential citizenship arrangements where actual adhesion to the Commonwealth is not contemplated, as, for instance, with the United States, as Sir Winston Churchill once suggested. A similar arrangement with Greece in respect of Cyprus might serve as a practical way of meeting the sentimental agitation for union with Greece without depriving the island of the advantages of its position in the Commonwealth.

These various changes in the structure of the Commonwealth have inevitably affected both the position of the Crown and its appropriate designation in each member nation. The uniformity of title, agreed upon by the Imperial Conference of 1926, still prevailed at the time of the Queen's accession, subject, however, to the omission, in 1947, by agreement of all the parliaments concerned, of the words 'Empress of India'. It then stood as follows:

'Elizabeth the Second, by the Grace of God, of Great Britain, Ireland and of the British Dominions beyond the Seas Queen, Defender of the Faith.'

The preamble of the Statute of Westminster declared that any alteration in the law touching the succession to the Throne or the Royal Style and Titles should require the assent of the parliaments of all the Dominions as well as of the parliament of the United Kingdom. It was obvious, when the Prime Ministers in Conference last autumn came to consider the matter, that certain changes were required in order to meet the new conditions. Ireland, as such, was no longer in the picture. India could only be covered by bringing in the new designation 'Head of the Commonwealth'. 'Defender of the Faith', applicable by a stretch to all Christian member nations, could hardly apply to the new Hindu, Moslem, and Buddhist members. The growing dislike of any term even remotely suggesting any kind of supremacy on the part of this country had already led to the dropping of the adjective British as descriptive of a Commonwealth now so largely Asian in its membership. Similarly the term 'Dominion' had tended to become regarded in some quarters as implying British domination or, at any rate, a status somehow inferior to that of an independent nation. The fine old word 'Realm' suggested itself as equally applicable to the United Kingdom and as emphasizing the direct relation of each member, other than the Indian Republic, to the Crown.

Whether it would have been possible to have agreed upon a new uniform title embodying these changes is doubtful. Anyhow it was decided that it would be in accord with the developments in the constitutional position since the preamble of the Statute of Westminster, that each member country should use for its own purposes a form of title which suited its own particular circumstances, but also retained a substantial element which was common to all. For the United Kingdom the title now stands:

'Elizabeth the Second, by the Grace of God of the United Kingdom of Great Britain and Northern Ireland and of her other Realms and Territories Queen, Head of the Commonwealth, Defender of the Faith.'

Canada, Australia, and New Zealand have followed closely, only inserting their own particular Realm after the United Kingdom. South Africa and Ceylon leave out the reference to the United Kingdom. Pakistan includes the United Kingdom, but without reference to Pakistan, no doubt in view of the probability of Pakistan following India's example and declaring itself a republic. None of these three includes 'Defender of the Faith', two for very obvious reasons.

The new titles have revived the somewhat metaphysical controversy as to the divisibility of the Crown. It has, of course, long been divisible in so far as its aspect and functions differ in each Realm. It is now still further divisible as between its constitutional aspect as an integral element in the constitution of each Realm and its symbolic aspect as carrying with it the Headship of the Commonwealth. But it is still a single, indivisible historic Crown following a single principle of succession and playing a more or less identical part in each constitution: a Crown whose wearer will at her Coronation dedicate herself equally to all her peoples in the terms of the same agreed oath. There is no resemblance here to the former personal union between the Crown of the United Kingdom and of Hanover, following different rules of succession and exercising widely different constitutional functions in the two kingdoms. It is a jewel of many facets, not a string of disconnected pearls.

A student of the purely formal structure of the Commonwealth might well be tempted by the record of constitutional developments, both before and since the war, to conclude that the Commonwealth itself is in process of tactful dissolution by mutual consent. He might, indeed, be confirmed in that conclusion by the evidence of diverging attitudes on the part of its members on issues of foreign policy, by acute differences between members over such questions as Kashmir, or the position of Indians in South Africa, or by the crude fact that the United Kingdom no longer enjoys that undisputed sea power under the shelter of which the Commonwealth grew and which, up to the last war, still held it together. But there is another side to the picture. Never has the process of mutual consultation and conference been more continuous or more practical. Since the war Prime Ministers have met in conference five times and are due to meet again at the time of the Coronation. There have been meetings of Finance Ministers and Defence Ministers, conferences on the peace settlement with Japan, or on Foreign Affairs generally, meetings of the Commonwealth Consultative Committee on the following up of the Colombo Plan for the development of South and South East Asia, ministerial and official meetings to discuss supply and production, official scientific, agricultural, and social insurance conferences, a conference of Commonwealth Speakers and, not least important, meetings of the Commonwealth Parliamentary Association. These meetings have taken place, not only in London but also in Ottawa, Canberra, Sydney, Wellington, and Colombo. All this over and above the continuous stream of information and consultation both by cable and by personal contact through High Commissioners.

If the Commonwealth is, not so much what it professes to be or not to be, as what it thinks, feels, and does, we may still be justified in believing that it will not only continue to hold together, but increasingly become an effective instrument for the development of the well being of all its members, for their common security, and for the maintenance of world peace. It may well be that the logical working out of the principles of separate independence and formal equality of status, which originated in the era of undisputed British naval supremacy, may have reached its limits, and may, under the economic and military pressures of a shrinking world, increasingly be replaced by a sense of the need for closer and more effective co-operation. It may then even become possible for the Governments of the Commonwealth to free themselves from that anti-Downing-Street complex which has survived from the past, and to recognize the practical advantages for the transaction of Commonwealth business of that more regularized continuity of conferences and that minimum of secretarial and technical machinery which they have had no hesitation in accepting in connexion with the United Nations, with the North Atlantic Treaty Organization or with the Council of Europe.

The nature of the Commonwealth association and of our obligations towards it has, indeed, been actively challenged by the development of the movement for European unity. This country's interest in the security of Europe, in face of the common danger from the East, and in the economic recovery of Europe, is obvious. No less obvious is the fact that we share intimately in the political and cultural tradition which Europe has inherited from Palestine, Greece, and Rome. It was only right that our interdependence with Europe was recognized by our taking part in the Council of Europe established in 1949. That body, though composed of a Council of Ministers representing the several Governments and an Assembly composed of delegates from the several Parliaments, is, in spite of its formal appearance, purely consultative. Its actual powers are no greater than those of conferences of Commonwealth Ministers or of the Commonwealth Parliamentary Association. There is no inconsistency between the United Kingdom's participation in the Council's deliberations and its prior responsibilities to its partners in the Commonwealth.

The difficulty only arises from the desire of some, at least, of the European Governments to transform the nations participating in the Council of Europe, or an inner group among them, into a federal or quasi-federal system involving the definite and irrevocable surrender of some part of their sovereignty by each of its component nations to a central government. Such a surrender

would run counter to the whole basis of our Commonwealth relations, resting as they do on the co-operation
of fully sovereign Governments. Our relation to such
a federal system, if it should come into being, could
still be close. But it would be, like that of Canada to
the United States, outside its constitutional structure.
On the other hand, so long as the development of
European unity proceeds on the Commonwealth
principle of free consultation without surrender of
sovereignty, that principle is sufficiently elastic to
permit of a wide measure of interlocking between the
two groups. That interlocking is, in any case, dictated,
in the circumstances of the time, by urgent considerations of defence. Last October's resolution of the
Strasbourg Assembly in favour of interlocking preferential tariffs between Europe and the Commonwealth
indicates a practical method of dealing with the no
less urgent common problem of the dollar gap and of
the restoration of exchange convertibility. It is in the
relationship of the Commonwealth as a whole to
Europe as a whole, rather than in those of this country
to Europe, that both the defensive and the economic
problems can best find their solution.

I turn to the domestic aspect of our constitution.
Sir Harold Nicolson's *Life of King George V* has now
provided invaluable information on the position and
influence of the Monarch in a period of recurring
constitutional crisis. He brings out the extent of the
pressure put on the King by Mr. Asquith's Cabinet,
under threat of resignation, to give a secret pledge to
over-ride the House of Lords by the creation of
additional peers in the hypothetical event of a Liberal

victory at the second 1910 election. We now know, for the first time, how earnestly the King in his relations with Mr. Asquith exercised his right of warning against the danger of the drift to civil war over Ireland, and with what complacent optimism his warnings were disregarded. The second of these letters of warning, that of September 1913, deserves to be read in full, not only for the wisdom and prescience with which it discussed the immediate situation, but for its firm insistence on the Sovereign's 'undoubted right to change his advisers' and dissolve, acting (to quote Erskine May), 'in the interest of the State and on grounds which could be justified to Parliament'. No less important, in its constitutional aspect, is the draft letter, never actually dispatched in view of the imminence of war, asking for a 'statement of the full and considered reasons' which impelled Ministers to ask for his assent to the Home Rule Bill, a measure which reached him as 'the result of a drastic, though as yet incomplete, change in the British Constitution'.

It is enough here to refer to the King's part in bringing about the abortive conference which broke down over the boundaries of Ulster, to his activities in the war, to his influence upon the opening of the negotiations with the Irish leaders which led to the setting up of the Irish Free State, and to his direct intervention in favour of a coalition in the economic crisis of 1931. Sir Harold Nicolson's account of these great matters, and of much else of lesser consequence, should dispel the idea that the Monarch is a purely passive element in the Constitution, however much his powers are normally limited by constitutional usage and sufferance.

An issue bearing on the constitutional powers of the Crown, which I only touched on in my lectures (see page 7) in connexion with the controversy between Lord Byng and Mr. Mackenzie King in 1926, is the right of the Sovereign to reject a Prime Minister's demand for a dissolution if an alternative Government can be formed in the same Parliament. So far as the other Realms—to use the new terminology—are concerned, the precedent of Sir Patrick Duncan's refusal in 1939 of a dissolution to General Hertzog and his calling upon General Smuts to form a government, is conclusive. But it has been suggested that this is not the case here, inasmuch as there is no instance of such a refusal for over a century. Mr. Asquith, however, was clearly of the contrary opinion. On 18 December 1923, when it was evident that no one Party would have a majority in the House of Commons, he stated his view of the position as follows:

'The notion that a Minister who cannot command a majority in the House of Commons is invested with a right to demand a dissolution is as subversive of constitutional usage as it would, in my opinion, be pernicious to the paramount interests of the nation.'

This statement was made by Mr. Asquith in view of his intention to put the Socialist Party into power and, presumably, with the idea that if it failed he might be in a position to take office with Conservative support. Sir Harold Nicolson now confirms the doctrine of the unexhausted utility of Parliament advanced by Mr. Asquith, for he makes it clear that the King granted the dissolution asked for by Mr. MacDonald with the utmost reluctance, and only after ascertaining from the leaders of the Conservative and Liberal Parties that they were unable or unwilling to form an administration.

The most important change in the Constitution since the war was brought about by the Parliament Act of 1949. The Parliament Act of 1911 was regarded by its authors as a permanent settlement, so far as the powers enjoyed by the House of Lords were concerned. The principle upon which it was based was the right of a House of Commons to secure the passage of any legislation passed in its first three sessions while still, presumably, expressing the 'mandate' of the electorate. In order to prevent this principle being defeated by extending the life of Parliament, any such extension was specifically excluded from the provisions of the Act. By a curious oversight it does not seem to have been realized that the intention of the Act could be equally well defeated by legislation under the Act reducing the delay of three successive sessions and two years stipulated in the Act. This unforeseen loophole was utilized by Mr. Attlee's Government in October 1947 to introduce a new Parliament Bill shortening the three sessions to two and the two years to one. As the year counts from the first Second Reading of a measure which might not reach the House of Lords for the first time in its final shape as much as eight months later, the power of delay was, in fact, so reduced as to be almost worthless. The measure was not, like the Act of 1911, the result of a deadlock and a subsequent election, but purely preventive. As a matter of dictatorial convenience it was even made retrospective in respect of legislation introduced before it became law. The House of Lords has, in substance, been deprived

of all powers and functions except that of debating at
large and of scrutinizing legislation and suggesting
such amendments as may commend themselves to the
Government of the day.

Before so revolutionary a measure was passed an
effort was made at a private conference between the
leaders of the three Parties to see whether it might not
be possible to come to an agreed settlement, both upon
the composition and the powers of the Upper House,
which they could recommend to their respective Parties.
So far as the composition was concerned, agreement
was reached on the general principle of a non-hereditary,
non-elective House composed of individuals, including
women, nominated on the strength of their personal
distinction or public service. These were to be styled
Lords of Parliament. It was further agreed that the
Second Chamber should be complementary to and
not a rival of the House of Commons, and that it should
not be so constituted as to give a permanent majority
to any political party. Peers who were not nominated
as Lords of Parliament to be free to stand for election
to the House of Commons and to vote like other
citizens. There should be some remuneration so
that no one should be excluded for lack of means. Even
as to powers the difference was narrowed down to a few
months. The Conservatives maintained that the whole
intention of the Act of 1911, whose principle they did
not dispute, was that a seriously controversial measure,
on which the view of the electorate was doubtful, should
not 'pass into law until sufficient time had elapsed to
enable the electorate to be properly informed of the
issues involved and for public opinion to crystallize
and express itself'. The utmost they could accept, to

facilitate a general agreement, was a year from the first Third Reading in the House of Commons. The Socialist leaders were not prepared to go further than nine months, insisting that the House of Commons must be free to pass any legislation it wished in its fourth session. The Liberals were prepared to accept this, and the Conservatives might have been well advised to concur. For they would have either secured the essential of an agreed reform of the composition of the Upper House or else, as seems probable, been in the advantageous position of seeing the advice of the Socialist leaders rejected by their own back benches, who were already openly protesting against any change which would strengthen the moral authority of the Upper House and might, consequently, some day lead to general acceptance of an increase in its powers.

This cynical attitude emerged even more strongly in the refusal of the Party in February 1953 to allow their leaders to accept Sir Winston Churchill's invitation for a renewal of the discussion of the general problem. That invitation was, in fact, stimulated by the introduction by Lord Simon of a simple measure authorizing the creation of not more than ten life peers, men or women, in any one year. His Bill, for the moment, stands adjourned, pending the introduction of more comprehensive proposals by the Government. But if, for one reason or another, the opportunity for a wider scheme of reform is once more allowed to be lost, it is sincerely to be hoped that Lord Simon's modest proposal will find its place on the Statute Book, for it breaks the ice in asserting a principle which is bound, sooner or later, to transform the situation.

The tendency towards egalitarian democracy was carried to its final limit by the Representation of the People Act of 1948. The Speaker's Conference which reported in 1944 had agreed upon general redistribution, the abolition of double member constituencies, and the assimilation of the parliamentary and local government franchise. But it had retained the University seats, the two members for the City of London and the business vote. These three features were now abolished in disregard of the constitutional convention by which the Parties have hitherto considered themselves as under a moral obligation to accept the agreed recommendations of the Speaker's Conference, at any rate for a reasonable number of years. Incidentally it deprived British graduates living abroad and alien graduates of a right previously enjoyed. The principle of 'one man one vote', though not that of 'one vote, one value', was thus finally established. The abolition of the University constituencies has, indeed, ended the one very limited experiment in Proportional Representation which had been introduced into our parliamentary system. At the same time the new electorate would seem in the last two elections to have controverted one of the arguments against Proportional Representation, namely that the existing system has the merit of ensuring substantial working majorities.

The tendency to overwork Parliament has continued unchecked. In the first post-war Parliament this was mainly due to the enormous volume of legislation which the Government was determined to force through the legislative sausage machine. In 1947, apart from two Budgets and their consequential embodiment in legislation, half a dozen major measures were passed, any one of which would, before 1939, have been considered a fair session's work. There was the Agriculture Act, the Transport Act, the Town and Country Planning Act (with a similar measure for Scotland), the Electricity Act, and the Scottish Health Service Act. Several of these were not only highly controversial, but also highly complicated and indefinite in respect of the powers conferred. To enable Parliament to get through such a spate of legislation it was found necessary not only to take most major bills in Standing Committee upstairs but also to apply the guillotine in Standing Committee, as well as in Committee of the whole House.

Since 1950 it has no longer been possible to send important controversial bills upstairs, for the simple reason that the proportional composition of the Standing Committee would have left the Government with no working majority. Today the over-working of Parliament is due less to the mass of legislation, though even this is still formidable, than to the smallness of majorities and the consequent imperative necessity which obliges members to be in constant attendance. The rigid disciplining of attendance involved has tended to be accompanied by a corresponding rigidity in the disciplining of opinion. The recent decision of the Socialist Party to forbid the existence of groups within the Party must be disquieting for all who believe that freedom of discussion is of the very essence of our constitution.

Meanwhile the process of controlling, by legislation, the everyday life of the citizen, whether as a producer or as a consumer, and, as an inevitable consequence, by delegated legislation and extra-judicial interpretation, has gone on steadily. Typical of the tendency of the age was the Supplies and Services (Transitional Powers) Act 1945 by which the wartime apparatus of subordinate law-making was switched over to the peacetime purposes of

'So maintaining, controlling and regulating supplies and services as to secure a sufficiency of those essential to the well-being of the community or their equitable distribution or their availability at fair prices, or . . . to facilitate the readjustment of industry and commerce to the requirements of the community in times of peace.'

Even these powers were not thought wide enough and were expanded in 1947 as to afford scope for

'promoting the productivity of industry, commerce and agriculture . . . and generally for ensuring that the whole resources of the community are available for use, and are used, in a manner best calculated to serve the interests of the community.'

It is under legislation of this blanket character that in 1948 Orders of different kinds were being issued at the rate of fifty-five a week with more than three hundred officials in eighteen departments having power to sign them. In much of this legislation the citizen who may have suffered serious damage to his property or to his livelihood has no appeal but from one official to another. A Select Committee was set up in December 1952 to consider in what respects the control of Parliament over delegated legislation could be improved. This will, no doubt, take into consideration Sir Gilbert (Lord) Campion's suggestion that the Statutory Instruments Committee which was set up in 1946 should be empowered to report, not only on the forms

of departmental action incidental to delegated legislation, but also on grievances arising out of their actual
operation. Meanwhile amid all the vast volume of
bureaucratic legislation and quasi-judicial interpretation there stands out at least 'one good deed in a
naughty world'. The Crown Proceedings Act of 1947
was a long overdue reform which substantially removed
the unfairness of the situation in which, through the
combination of two legal maxims—one that the King
cannot be impleaded in his own Courts and the other
that he can do no wrong—the citizen could not sue the
Crown in tort, and could only sue it in contract by a
special procedure through petition of right. The
immunity of the Crown is, however, retained in respect
of the Armed Forces, so far as concerns actions brought
by members of those Forces in respect of injuries
attributable to service for entitlement to pension, and,
as regards the Post Office, in relation to unregistered
postal packets and telephonic communications.

So far as the procedure of the House of Commons is
concerned new Standing Orders were introduced in
1947. In order to speed up legislation the limit on the
number of Standing Committees was removed, their
quorum lowered, and, as I have already mentioned, the
guillotine made applicable to their discussions. The
discussion of finance was speeded up by consolidating
the debate on the Budget resolutions, in effect by cutting
out the duplication of debate on the financial resolution
and in the Finance Bill itself. The number of supply
days was increased from twenty to twenty-six, an
extension still by no means commensurate with the ever
wider range of subjects to be discussed. On the other
hand, since 1950 private members have had their

Fridays restored for legislation and motions alternately, while retaining the half-hour debate on the Motion to Adjourn at the end of each night's debate, which was introduced in the war. These debates, as often as not, arise out of question time and constitute in some sort an extension of it. They are, in a sense, typical of the way in which the function of the House as a tribunal of review is growing in importance as its control over legislation by effective detailed discussion has been weakened.

One major problem of parliamentary review and ministerial control for which no satisfactory solution has yet been found is that presented by the statutory boards in charge of various nationalized industries. These have been set up in order to meet the criticism that Civil Service administration, with its cautious routine methods and its pre-occupation with records to protect Ministers against parliamentary criticism, could not provide the continuous stimulus to efficiency, adaptability, and enterprise which the prospect of profit or loss applies to private industry. On the other hand, the chief justification of nationalization is the argument that a nationalized industry can be directed to serve broader national interests, even at the expense of its own immediate financial advantage. The immediate interest of the coal industry, for instance, may well be to sell coal at the highest price which the consuming industries and public will pay, and not to open new mines unless they can clearly pay their way. But the interests of industry at large might be held to justify the present practice of the Coal Board of selling at a price fixed by the average cost of production, or even justify selling at a loss, while the need for abundant power might warrant the opening of more new mines than the coal industry, as a self-regarding industry, might think worth while.

Obviously, therefore, Ministers must retain control over the general policy of nationalized industries, while it is within the limits of their general ministerial directives that the administrative boards must follow the ordinary methods of competitive industry. But the line of demarcation between general policy and administration is not always easy. The board of a public corporation may have strong objections on practical grounds to a policy favoured by a Minister. The Minister's power of appointing or dismissing the personnel of the board, and of supplying or withholding finance, may not always be easy to exercise, and may create political difficulties of a very different kind from those involved in over-ruling the Civil Service. In any case, no Minister is likely to try to enforce a policy upon a nationalized industry without fully informing himself as to its working. This he must naturally delegate in large measure to his department, with a consequent tendency to extend Civil Service methods into the working of the industry itself. Much depends on the personal factor. An able and enterprising Minister may exercise the same kind of general direction and stimulation that the chairman of a great business organization can exercise on the board of a subsidiary company. But the opportunities for friction, and still more for inertia, are there, and the general tendency of Ministers is apt to be one of acceptance of a board's view, on policy as well as on administration, and of defence of it when challenged in Parliament.

The Ministerial aspect of control, though intrinsically more important, has been less discussed than
the parliamentary aspect. There is first of all the
problem of what questions with regard to the administration of a public corporation may be addressed to
Ministers, and how far Ministers are entitled to refuse
to answer on the ground that a question is concerned
only with day to day management, and not with policy.
The solution imposed by Mr. Speaker Clifton Brown
in 1948 was that he would be the judge of whether a
question upon which information had been refused,
should be allowed as being 'of sufficient public importance'. On the other hand, the Report of the Select
Committee on Nationalized Industries recommended
in October 1952 that the onus of deciding whether
a question should be placed upon the Order Paper,
should not rest upon the Clerks at the Table, but
that, unless obviously repetitive or dealing with
matters of administrative detail, it should go forward, leaving it for the Minister to give or refuse
an answer.

Debates on the adjournment may cover a somewhat
wider ground than questions. The Government can
offer special days to discuss the work of individual cor-
porations or the Opposition can select them for supply
days. But such discussions, while they can challenge
policy as a whole, or serve as a check on obvious instances of inefficiency, can do little to stimulate positive
efficiency or initiative. Special parliamentary committees, such as I have suggested elsewhere (see page
33) to secure better informed criticism of the work of
departments, might be of real service, even if open to
the charge of placing fresh burdens on over-worked

members and Ministers. The extension of nationalization would certainly strengthen the case for a House of
Industry with the time and the trained outlook which
would qualify it for the purpose in view. A simpler and,
in most cases, preferable solution, is to leave industry in
private hands, but to let Government make far bolder
use than in the past of financial incentives and dis-
incentives in order to direct private enterprise into
nationally desirable channels.

But what are the desirable channels? That brings us
back at once to the main issues of policy and to the
efficiency of the Cabinet as an instrument not only for
co-ordinating the work of departments but, even more
important, for co-ordinating it in the light of what the
Haldane Report called 'the duty of investigation and
thought as preliminary to action'. The most that can
be said on this subject is that the last few years have
seen an increasing recognition of the importance of the
problem, but no systematic effort to deal with it.
Co-ordination, in the negative sense of the adjustment
of current differences between departments, has
undoubtedly been improved by the development of the
system of standing and *ad hoc* committees of the Cabinet.
On the more positive—what one might call the General
Staff or Planning side—the one definite advance since
the war has been the retention of the Ministry of
Defence, on the lines developed by Sir Winston
Churchill, as a permanent department in charge of a
Minister of Defence, with a relatively small planning
and co-ordinating staff drawn from the three Services.

A further and no less urgently needed advance was
begun by Mr. Attlee when he appointed Sir Stafford
Cripps Minister for Economic Affairs in September

1947. But the experiment was, in fact, abandoned six weeks later, when Sir Stafford Cripps was made Chancellor of the Exchequer and general economic policy became once more subordinate to the Treasury, strengthened by the addition of an Economic Secretary (temporarily raised to the status of a Minister of State for Economic Affairs while held by Sir Arthur Salter from November 1951 to February 1953). Nothing that has happened in these years has, to my mind, diminished the objections which I have voiced in Chapter III (pages 94–97) to the undue predominance thus given to considerations of purely fiscal and financial policy as compared with those of production and productive efficiency.

Sir Winston Churchill's Cabinet is, at the time of writing (April 1953), of the same general size as Mr. Attlee's—seventeen as against sixteen. It includes six members of the House of Lords, of whom only one, Lord Swinton, is in charge of an ordinary department —Commonwealth Relations—Lord Alexander being in charge of Defence. Of the other three, Lord Woolton and Lord Leathers were specifically designated as co-ordinators, the first of Agriculture and Food and the second of Transport and Fuel and Power. These designations created a good deal of speculation and criticism as to the exact powers and responsibilities of these 'Overlords', speculation and criticism which might have been avoided if they had been simply described as Ministers without administrative departments, but informally charged with keeping an eye on certain aspects of policy, in addition to the wider functions of general advice which, no doubt, was Sir Winston Churchill's main reason for including them in his Cabinet.[1] Lord Cherwell, nominally Paymaster-General, offers, perhaps, the nearest approach to that function of general thinking ahead, especially in matters of scientific research, which is still so inadequately represented in our Cabinet system, and in doing so maintains a close personal association which Sir Winston Churchill has long found helpful. The Cabinet has, in fact, been largely built, as it always must be to some extent, on personal lines. But the problem of a more efficient structure for the framing and co-ordination of policy still remains to be solved.

[1] Sir Winston Churchill dealt with the matter in a full statement on 6 May 1952 in which he drew a clear distinction between the general Ministerial responsibility of these co-ordinating Ministers—which in no way impaired or diminished the responsibility of the Departmental Ministers—and the statutory powers of the Minister of Defence.

BIBLIOGRAPHY

AMERY, L. S. *The Forward View.*
AMERY, L. S. *My Political Life.*
ANDERSON, SIR J. *The Machinery of Government* (Romanes Lecture, 1946).
ANSON, SIR W. *The Law and Custom of the Constitution.*
ATTLEE, EARL. *A Prime Minister Remembers (Edited by* FRANCIS WILLIAMS).
ATTLEE, EARL. *Empire into Commonwealth.*
AVON, LORD. *Memoirs: Full Circle.*
BAGEHOT, W. *The English Constitution (Introd. by* R. H. S. CROSSMAN).
BARKER, SIR ERNEST. *Reflections on Government. Essays on Government.*
BURKE, EDMUND. *Writings and Speeches.*
CAMPION, LORD (and others). *Parliament: A Survey.*
CAMPION, LORD (and others). *British Government since 1918.*
CARTER, B. C. *The Office of Prime Minister.*
CECIL, LADY GWENDOLEN. *Life of Lord Salisbury.*
CHESTER, D. N. and WILLSON, F. M. G. *The Organisation of British Central Government.*
COURTNEY OF PENWITH, LORD. *The Working Constitution of the United Kingdom.*
CRIPPS, SIR S. (and others). *Problems of a Socialist Government.*
DAALDER, H. *Cabinet Reform in Britain 1914–62.*
DALTON, H. *Memoirs: 1945–60.*
DICEY, A. V. *Introduction to the Study of the Law of the Constitution.*
DISRAELI, BENJAMIN. *Vindication of the English Constitution.*
EHRMAN, J. *Cabinet Government and War 1890–1940.*
FINER, H. *Representative Government and the Parliament of Industry.*
HALL, DUNCAN. *British Commonwealth of Nations.*
HANKEY, LORD. *Diplomacy by Conference.*
HANSARD SOCIETY. *Parliamentary Affairs* (annual articles on the Constitution).
HANSARD SOCIETY. *Parliamentary Reform 1933–60.*
HEARN, A. *The Government of England.*
HEMINGFORD, LORD. *Backbencher and Chairman.*
HOLLAND, BERNARD. *Life of the Duke of Devonshire.*
JEBB, R. *The Imperial Conference.*
JENNINGS, SIR W. IVOR. *Cabinet Government. Parliament.*
KEITH, A. B. *Responsible Government in the Dominions. Speeches and Documents on the British Dominions, 1918–31.*
LASKI, H. J. *Democracy in Crisis.*
LASKI, H. J. *Reflections on the Constitution.*
LATHAM, SIR J. G. *Australia and the British Commonwealth.*
LOW, SIDNEY. *The Governance of England.*
LOWELL, A. LAWRENCE. *The Government of England.*
MACKINDER, SIR H. J. *Democracy and Reality.*
MACKINTOSH, J. P. *The British Cabinet.*
MANSERGH, N. *Documents and Speeches on British Commonwealth Affairs 1931–52.*
MILL, J. S. *Representative Government.*
MILLER, J. D. P. *The Commonwealth in the World.*
MONTESQUIEU. *L'Esprit des Lois.*
MORRISON OF LAMBETH, LORD. *Autobiography.*
MORRISON OF LAMBETH, LORD. *Government and Parliament.*
MUIR, J. RAMSAY. *How Britain is Governed.*
NICOLSON, SIR HAROLD. *King George V.*
NICOLSON, N. *People and Parliament.*
OXFORD AND ASQUITH, EARL OF. *Fifty Years of Parliament.*
PERCY, LORD EUSTACE. *Government in Transition.*
PICKTHORN, KENNETH. *Some Historical Principles of the Constitution.*
SALTER, SIR A. *The Framework of an Ordered Society.*
SEELEY, SIR J. *Introduction to Political Science.*
STANNARD, HAROLD. *The Two Constitutions.*
TAYLOR, SIR H. *The Statesman.*
WEBB, SIDNEY AND BEATRICE. *Constitution for the Socialist Commonwealth of Great Britain.*
WHEARE, K. C. *Government by Committee.*
WHEELER-BENNETT, SIR JOHN. *King George VI, His Life and Reign.*

INDEX

*Printed lithographically
by Jarrold and Sons Ltd
Norwich*